WRITERS AND THEIR WORK

ISOBEL ARMSTRONG
*General Editor*

# MATTHEW ARNOLD

# MATTHEW ARNOLD

Kate Campbell

First published in 2008 by Northcote House Publishers Ltd, Horndon, Tavistock, Devon, PL19 9NQ, United Kingdom.
Tel: +44 (0) 1822 810066  Fax: +44 (0) 1822 810034.

**British Library Cataloguing-in-Publication Data**
A catalogue record for this book is available from the British Library

ISBN 978-0-7463-1034-2 hardcover
ISBN 978-0-7463-0946-9 paperback

Typeset by PDQ Typesetting, Newcastle-under-Lyme
Printed and bound in the United Kingdom

# Contents

# Acknowledgements

My thanks to the UEA readers of drafts of this book, Jon Cook, Tim Marshall and Clive Scott.

# Biographical Outline

| | |
|---|---|
| 1822 | December 24, Matthew Arnold born at Laleham-on-Thames: first son, second child of nine surviving children of Thomas and Mary Arnold |
| 1828 | Family move to Rugby School where Thomas Arnold becomes Headmaster as Dr Arnold |
| 1837 | Enters Rugby School |
| 1841 | Goes up to Balliol College, Oxford; Thomas Arnold appointed Regius Professor of Modern History |
| 1842 | Thomas Arnold dies |
| 1844 | Awarded BA |
| 1845 | February – April, an assistant master at Rugby School |
| | Elected fellow, Oriel College, Oxford |
| 1847 | Appointed Private Secretary to Lord Lansdowne |
| 1848 | February, visits Paris during Revolution |
| | Autumn, on holiday in Switzerland: 'Marguerite' poems appear to be based on an encounter here |
| 1849 | February, *The Strayed Reveller and Other Poems* (published anonymously, by 'A') |
| | Autumn, on holiday in Switzerland, where he begins 'Marguerite' poems |
| 1850 | Elder sister, Jane, marries W.E. Forster (who became a Liberal MP and Minister of Education in 1868) |
| | April, appointed inspector of schools |
| 1851 | June, marries Frances Lucy Wightman |
| | October, begins work as a schools' inspector |
| 1852 | First son born |
| | October, *Empedocles on Etna and Other Poems* (by 'A'). |
| 1853 | Northcote-Trevelyan Report on the civil service |
| | Second son born |
| | November, *Poems: A New Edition* (with acknowledgement |

vii

of Arnold's authorship, and with his major poetic statement in the 'Preface')

1854    Crimean War
        December, *Poems: Second Series*

1855    Third son born
        Abolition of the Stamp Duty on newspapers

1856    Joins Athenæum Club

1857    May, elected Professor of Poetry at Oxford (appointment renewed in 1862 for a further five years)
        November, delivers inaugural lecture, 'On the Modern Element in Literature'

1858    Establishes first independent residence, Chester Square, London
        First daughter born

1859    March-August, travel in France, Holland, Switzerland, on Newcastle Commission on elementary education
        August, publication of first free-standing criticism, a pamphlet on 'England and the Italian Question'

1861    January, *On Translating Homer* (following delivery of three lectures at Oxford)
        May, *The Popular Education of France*, with 'Democracy' as its introduction
        Second daughter born
        Death of Arthur Hugh Clough
        July, Robert Lowe produces the Revised Code at end of the parliamentary session

1862    March, first journal publication, 'The Twice Revised Code' in *Fraser's Magazine*

1863    January, 'The Bishop and the Philosopher' in *Macmillan's Magazine*

1864    June, *A French Eton* (the collection of three essays from *Macmillan's Magazine*, September 1863, February and May 1864)

1865    February, *Essays in Criticism* (after journal publication of essays, January 1863–November 1864)
        April-November, travel in France, Italy, Germany and Switzerland on Taunton Commission
        October, death of Palmerston

1866    February, 'My Countrymen', in *Cornhill Magazine*
        Fourth son born

1867    June, *On the Study of Celtic Literature* (first published in the

*Cornhill*, March, April, May, July, 1866)
July, 'Culture and Its Enemies', *Cornhill* (after delivery as last lecture of Oxford Professorship)
*New Poems*
August, Reform Act receives royal assent: extension of the franchise

1868 January, death of infant son
March, *Schools and Universities on the Continent*
November, death of oldest child at sixteen
December, W.E. Gladstone becomes Prime Minister for the first time
January, *Culture and Anarchy* (first published as essays in *Cornhill Magazine*, July 1867, then five more essays February–September, 1868)
Irish Church disestablished
Endowed Schools Act, a significant step in state support of secondary education

1870 *Saint Paul and Protestantism*
Elementary Education Act (sometimes known as 'Forster's Education Act', requires local authorities to provide elementary education)

1871 *Friendship's Garland*
Abolition of university tests – ends exclusion of nonconformists from the ancient universities

1872 Death of eighteen-year-old son

1873 *Literature and Dogma*
Death of Mary Arnold
*God and the Bible*

1877 *Last Essays on Church and Religion*

1878 *Selected Poems of Matthew Arnold*

1879 *Mixed Essays*
*Poems of Wordsworth*
Start of Gladstone's high profile election campaign in Midlothian

1880 Education Act, introduces compulsory education

1881 *Poetry of Byron*

1882 *Irish Essays*

1883 Accepts civil list pension, pension for services to poetry and literature (in addition to normal salary, c £1000)
American tour

1884 Reform Act, extends franchise

1885 *Discourses in America*
1886 Second American tour
1887 Retires as inspector of schools
1888 April, dies of heart attack
     November *Essays in Criticism (Second Series)*

# Abbreviations and References

1 – 6    *The Letters of Matthew Arnold*, ed. Cecil Lang (Charlottes-
ville, Va.: University Press of Virginia, 1996–2001). Vol. 1,
1828–1859. Vol. 2, 1860–1865. Vol. 3, 1866–1870. Vol. 4,
1871–1878. Vol. 5, 1879–1884. Vol. 6, 1885–1888.

I – XI    *Complete Prose Works* of Matthew Arnold, ed. R. H. Super
(Ann Arbor: University of Michigan Press, 1960–1977).
Vol. I, *On the Classical Tradition*. Vol. II, *Democratic
Education*. Vol. III, *Lectures and Essays in Criticism*. Vol.
IV, *Schools and Universities on the Continent*. Vol. V, *Culture
and Anarchy with Friendship's Garland and some Literary
Essays*. Vol. VI, *Dissent and Dogma*. Vol. VII, *God and the
Bible*. Vol. VIII, *Essays Religious and Mixed*. Vol. IX, *English
Literature and Irish Politics*. Vol. X, *Philistinism in England
and America*. Vol. XI, *The Last Word*.

C&A      *Culture and Anarchy: an Essay in Social and Political
Criticism* by Matthew Arnold, ed. John Dover Wilson
(Cambridge: Cambridge University Press, 1988 [1932]).

CHP      *Matthew Arnold: The Poetry. The Critical Heritage*, ed. Carl
Dawson (London: Routledge & Kegan Paul, 1973).

CHPW     *Matthew Arnold: Prose Writings. The Critical Heritage*, ed.
Carl Dawson and John Pfordresher (London: Routledge,
1995).

L        *The Letters of Matthew Arnold to Arthur Hugh Clough*, ed. H.
F. Lowry (Oxford: Clarendon Press, 1932).

N        *The Notebooks of Matthew Arnold*, eds. Karl Young and
Hilary Waldo Dunn (London: Oxford University Press,
1952).

PP       *Parliamentary Papers: Reports of HM Inspectors of Schools
1852:LXXX*

P      *The Poems of Matthew Arnold,* eds. Kenneth Allott and Miriam Allott (London: Longman, 1979 [1965]).

S      *Reports on Elementary Schools,* ed. F. Sandford (London: Macmillan, 1889).

Y      *The Yale Manuscript,* ed. S.O.A. Ullmann (Ann Arbor: University Press of Michigan, 1989).

# Introduction

The aim and office of instruction, say many people, is to make a man a good citizen, or a good Christian, or a gentleman; or it is to enable him to do his duty in that state of life to which he is called. It is none of these, and the modern spirit more and more discerns it to be none of these. These are at best secondary aims of instruction; its prime object is to enable man *to know himself and the world*. Such knowledge is *the only sure basis for action*, and this basis it is the true aim and office of instruction to supply.

(My emphasis in second instance, IV: 290)

More than many writers, Matthew Arnold has generated opposing reactions for different readers and he resists simple classification. As a poet, he has been seen generally as significant although he has never been widely popular. As a critic, he remains a common reference point in literature, cultural studies and the humanities, although he is more subject to denigration than admiration. In the 1970s and 1980s, a number of English critics who were influenced by Marxism identified him as a thinker who sought to protect the interests of the propertied classes, both in his criticism of working-class politics and in his writing about the need to replace class allegiances with culture.[1] His absolutism and detachment are also a source of criticism today, and despite his appeal to some liberal thinkers he can readily appear an unsympathetic figure in a multicultural era on account of his insensitivity to cultural difference. To convey his absolutism, critics mention his authoritarian-sounding calls for 'force till right is ready', 'the best that has been known and thought in the world' (III: 266, 282), or his literary 'touchstones'; or they allude to Arnoldian culture, which is associated with exclusivity. On such grounds, his importance is now in question.[2]

1

From the 1930s to the 1960s his criticism was widely admired for a liberal humanism that values wholeness in the individual and seeing life whole. The influential English literary critic, F. R. Leavis, celebrated Arnold's democratic tendencies and ethical force, and one of the founders of English Cultural Studies, Raymond Williams, saw him as 'a great and important figure in nineteenth-century thought . . . we can hardly speak better than in his own best spirit'.[3] In mid-twentieth-century America a leading liberal critic, Lionel Trilling, also valued him as a humanist, and Arnold has remained an important figure for American intellectuals. In the mid-century decades, Williams and Trilling acknowledged Arnold's invidious social discriminations, yet this did not substantially qualify their regard.

In his lifetime, Arnold's reputation was a source of controversy. The sense of a liberal humanist was forestalled by an awareness of his taste for polemic and his elitism. In particular his claims on behalf of reason were seen to be in conflict with his self-promotion and prejudices. The Cambridge philosopher, Henry Sidgwick, saw the first part of Arnold's best known book, *Culture and Anarchy*, as a display of 'the delicate impertinences of egotism' by a man who was given to 'titillating the public by something like the airs and graces, the playful affectations of a favourite comedian' (*CHPW*: 210). Sidgwick fastened on the discrepancy between Arnold's 'profound truths' and his populist manner.

The disapproval that Arnold's journalistic methods incurred has faded from view and there is now little awareness that he was perceived as a reprehensible critic in his day. This introductory book foregrounds this aspect in the course of charting his life and work in relation to publicity until 1869 when *Culture and Anarchy* was published. Publicity's changing significance for Arnold appears here in his evolution as many different kinds of writer – a poet, a schools'-inspector-and-civil-servant who produces numerous reports, and a modern critic who moves between literary, social and political lectures, pamphlets, periodical essays and books. Publicity refers to the state of being open to public observation, and when Arnold first wrote of 'publicity' as a young poet at mid-century, the word especially denoted 'the exposure of one's thoughts and feelings to the general public' (Ullmann, *Y*: 173). Arnold's jotting observes how publicity undermines a sense of wholeness: 'No man can express more than one side at once...but he can have a feeling of the whole if he will not always be labouring after expression and publicity' (Y: 171, 172). The sense that a feeling of wholeness and adequate expression may depend on not paying attention to an audience echoes the nineteenth-century philosopher, John Stuart Mill. In his essay 'What is Poetry?', Mill maintained that poetry is utterance that is essentially 'overheard'. Publicity is here tied to philosophical issues about language and the self. Although Arnold indicates how he shuns publicity as a poet, his early poetry and private writing centre on the elusiveness of wholeness and the difficulty of communication.

When he became a schools' inspector, a civil servant and a critic, the value of a culture of publicity mostly overrode his personal anxieties about it. Indeed, according to the famous Arnoldian ideal, the 'great men of culture' spread 'the best knowledge, the best ideas' 'from one end of society to the other...yet still remaining the *best* knowledge and thought of the time' (V: 113). Echoes of the Enlightenment can be heard in this promotion of ideas and knowledge and, like Enlightenment philosophy, Arnold invoked publicity as a principle of good government in the 1860s. In this context it signals not only the discussion of ideas and the spread of information and standards, but also exposure to public scrutiny. In his administrative capacity, for instance, he urged 'publicity' for the proper management of schools (II: 42). His educational thinking developed through travel across national frontiers on fact-finding public inquiries into European schools, and this work bore out publicity's further, traditional association with a 'public', or international, world – as in the term 'public law'. The international aspect of publicity appears in Arnold's report on *Schools and Universities on the Continent* when it relates that an (unidentified) 'French publicist' has informed the Austrian Government of his idea of 'Modern States' (IV: 304–5).

Yet as a social and political critic who tried to influence readers, Arnold increasingly used instrumental forms of publicity that involved *making* something publicly known for particular purposes. From the late 1850s this kind of publicity was increasingly associated with journalism and it appears in this book as 'modern publicity'.[4] Arnold attracted the negative criticisms of this publicity that we have seen from Sidgwick and he uses the word 'publicist' negatively, in this sense, in 1867, when he describes the contemporary Positivist critic, Frederick Harrison, as a 'powerful young publicist, in full evening costume, furbishing up a guillotine. These things are very serious; and I say, if the masses are to have power, let them be instructed' (V: 76). This manipulative publicity was central to Arnold's activism, and when he writes about 'getting at' his readers (2: 238) he envisages action that goes beyond the impartial transmission of knowledge and ideas.

His use of publicity has meant that it can seem that his ideas are simply slogans. These ideas which appear in catchwords, and his attention to a range of modern issues, have contributed to his extraordinary continuing presence. As well as the Arnold of academic literary criticism, English in schools, cultural studies and Victorian poetry, there are the Arnolds of political thought, literary journalism and contemporary fiction.[5] In each of these fields his skills appear today in ideas and phrases that signal particular positions. The ideological Arnold who upholds 'disinterested' criticism has been central to the self-definition of cultural studies in their break from, or revision of, literary studies. In a recent essay that elaborates this role, Arnold appears as a 'master-strategist' who is 'largely responsible for establishing the discipline of "English"'.[6] Yet lengthy studies have tended to overlook the publicity-bearing, practical and power-seeking aspects of his work. And although briefer accounts mention his well-known catchwords and phrases, and even identify him as a publicist and strategist, they tend to gloss over his writing practice and his practical, political concerns. In these respects, postmodernism has scarcely caught up with Arnold and he remains something of an innocent – a strategist in a vacuum.

His critical career coincided with the development of modern media publicity from the mid-nineteenth century. Born in 1822, he wrote as a poet before he took up criticism. His poetry faces existential uncertainty, isolation and the dislocation of modern times. In the 1850s he sought to alleviate the cultural dislocation by working as a modern critic and a civil servant in education. The 'Preface' to his 1853 *Poems* maintains the importance of poetry and classical literature in lifting modern confusion. From

4

his inaugural lecture as Oxford Professor of Poetry in 1857, he advocated the study of rational methods as well as the importance of classical literature. His civil service employment led directly to political criticism – a little-known pamphlet about English, French and Italian politics in 1859, then an essay that sees education as fundamental to 'Democracy'. In his school work his contrasting allegiances to human 'spirit' and the contemporary world entail different kinds of liberalism - an aesthetic form of liberalism that values the arts, emotion and subjectivity, and a socio-political form that values reason, objectivity and the efficient modern state. From 1862 he published his criticism in journals as the form of publication that was best suited to diffusing ideas and exerting influence. Journalism was by then fundamental to party political activity and Arnold's most widely circulated literary essay, 'The Function of Criticism', and *Culture and Anarchy*, engage with contemporary politics significantly.

The chronological approach of the following account fore-grounds the interrelation-ship of Arnold's poetic sensibility, his professional work, contemporary journalism and politics in his evolution as a publicist. The story that unfolds is one of a writer whose many-sidedness lies not just within texts but also in his several identities and different kinds of publication. It indicates how these different roles need to be taken into account in assessing his prose, and in order to bring out its development his poetry is read in the order that it was written rather than published. Particular strands of this story include the changes in his literary style and the importance of 'the people' and the public, ideas, action, power and modernity in his writing and thinking. Until recently his social and political criticism has been related primarily to his anxieties over working-class disorder during riots that took place in Hyde Park in 1866. Here it will be read more pragmatically through post-structur-alist historical studies that indicate the role of language and the media from the 1850s in the inception of cultural politics, and also through liberal intellectual history. In 1994, the cultural critic Steven Marcus proposed Arnold's 'step toward the invention of cultural politics', and the work of recent historians indicates how the developments that Marcus describes were underway in the 1860s.

In this changing politics, 'cultural attitudes and preferences of sensibility come to stand for, take the place of, and finally become the functional equivalent of outright political preferences and arguments'.[7] The intellectual historian, Stefan Collini, foregrounds Arnold's concern with attitudes and sensibility, and the role of morality in late Victorian intellectual life generally. The following account links Arnold's moral sensibility to the new cultural politics as Collini's sense of his designs on his readers is developed in the light of Arnold's political commitment to state intervention.

The first chapter of this book outlines Arnold's emotional and literary formation, and his writing up until 1853. It reads his shift to criticism as a positive response to the version of modernity in his poetry, whereby he turned his back on self-preoccupation for commitment to rational action in society. The second chapter traces his idea of modernity and his publicist activity as he developed in different roles. Through his professional work as a civil servant in education he tried to advance a modern nation state, in advance of his famous writing about criticism and culture; and in 1857 he emerged as a critic who upholds standards for application across modern life. His publicist skills in conveying facts and ideas were exercised in writing general reports on the schools that he visited. The third chapter outlines his involvement in a new print culture and a new cultural politics, in which he became preoccupied with exerting influence as a writer through publicity. With remarkable versatility, he came to use journalism as a 'theatre of operations' for advancing his ideas. *Culture and Anarchy* not only develops his social and political ideas on a broad front, it also seeks to influence readers emotionally on the topical political issue of increased state intervention, which results in a rather anarchic text.

The range and volume of his work impose selectivity on all who write on Arnold, and this book of thirty-five thousand words ends in 1869 with this text that is the climax of his publicist activity. Almost all his well-known ideas had appeared by then. He wrote in a much more straightforward way in his books on religion in the 1870s, though ironically it was this writing that made him a celebrity. His modern publicist activity resumed after this religious spell of seven years, though by then his ideas and writing were less fresh, and his publicity ran on more routine lines where it was often tied to the interests of publishing houses. A brief postscript glances at this writing and his later life.

# 1

# Early Life, Poetry and Prose, 1822–1853

*The poet glances over the throng of orators, men of business & says –
how well might this and that man have been a poet: but the others do not
say vice versa* (Y: 98)

Matthew Arnold was always a creative and critical writer
although his writing life falls into two parts that centre on his
poetry and then his criticism. While he continued to write
poetry after the publication of his *Poems: a New Edition* in 1853,
this new collection marks his transition from poetry to criticism
since it was his third and last volume of poetry. Moreover its
'Preface' was the culmination of his poetic thinking. This
'Preface' repudiates the melancholy and 'dialogue of the mind
with itself' in modern poetry, yet many poems that Arnold had
written were distinguished by these features.[1] From his
appointment as Professor of Poetry at Oxford in 1857 he began
to write criticism that was more socially concerned and he
continued as a critic for the next thirty years. The significance of
his turn from poetry to criticism is, then, a central question
when considering his life and work. Not only is its meaning for
Arnold at issue but also broad questions about the self, literature
and society.

His change of direction was accentuated by his new employment and marriage in 1851. Biographers have tended to see a
transition from 'Romantic' creativity to 'Victorian' duty as a
husband, father and professional man.[2] Yet Arnold was not
straightforwardly a Romantic poet and his transition to criticism
can be seen in terms of his new commitment to rational action.
The American critic, J. Hillis Miller, in contrast elaborates his
'strategy of withdrawal from practical involvement' in his many

years of criticism. Miller's influential 1960s' account of a critic who 'must hover in the void . . . sternly and implacably criticising all present cultural forms as false' importantly perceives how the sense of fragmentation and emptiness in Arnold's poetry still continues in his criticism. His theological reading of writing that is marked by the disappearance of God has contributed to current readings of Arnold's detachment and his reference to Arnold's 'scrupulously empty phrases' is still much quoted.[3] Yet in foregrounding Arnold's 'withdrawal', Miller overlooks the secular redirection of his gaze in his turn to criticism.

Arnold saw a way forward from his sense of disconnection in his ideas about *praxis* and the shaping power of ideas before his work in education became important to him. He became a Schools Inspector in 1851 and this work was at the front of modern state intervention. The 'Preface' to his *New Edition* was also socially concerned. It was written in response to debate about poetry's social role and it attracted public notice. Arnold wrote that this 'Preface' demanded difficult new *'articulations'* (1: 276), and its publication signals his own articulation as a public man. His wide reputation as a writer dates from this essay and, in the basic sense of someone who puts forward ideas in public, he became a publicist then. From having been a source of great personal anxiety, publicity became something that he sought.

This chapter explores how Arnold moved from creative to critical writing and the importance of his early life, poetry and private writing for his later work as a critic. Criticism was always a likely destination for him, as many of his poems seem to lack strong poetic feeling in their 'dialogue of the mind with itself'. He will be seen moving away from their introspective mode towards a type of rational action that drew on the ancient Greek philosophy of Aristotle.

The public orbit of his father, Thomas Arnold, most obviously provided a grounding for Arnold's criticism through his work in the 'public' school, Rugby, and also in history, theology, the established Church, Oxford University and journalism. From his father Arnold gained early exposure to modern ideas and institutions as well as to the classics, and he serves here in sketching the context of Arnold's early work. Thomas was a publicist himself and his academic studies depended on publicity across national borders. Through his school sermons, and his antagonist, John Henry Newman – the Oxford cleric whose search for spiritual reformation led to conversion to Roman Catholicism in 1845 – Arnold encountered the force of religious prose especially. His mother, Mary Arnold, was also important to him in her differences from his father, including her Cornish descent and her love of poetry, though her role and further influences on Arnold are eclipsed in this brief book.

## UPBRINGING

Public and private spheres were hardly separated for Thomas Arnold and even in their time away from classrooms he tried to shape his children according to his ideas of public character. At sixteen he had gone up to Oriel College at Oxford University where he had developed radical and reforming interests as a member of a group called the Noetics. Less than ten years after his time at Oxford, as Dr Arnold, he moved on from his first teaching post in 1828 to become Headmaster of Rugby 'public' school where he sought reform through developing public spirit and Christian life in his pupils. Moral chaos and disorder prevailed in English public schools at the time. To overcome the anarchy at Rugby, Dr Arnold introduced a regime of religious observance and self-examination that was reinforced through surveillance by prefects in the sixth form. 'Moral thoughtfulness' was both agent and fruit of his pupils' transformation and it became second nature for many as they internalized the school's values. In the self-scrutiny and general questioning that Dr Arnold demanded, the 'dialogue of the mind with itself' was experienced in the fabric of daily life. Dr Arnold's own forceful character was also a significant influence on his pupils, so that his training in disinterest, or selflessness, worked through example as well as supervision, despite some arbitrariness in his rule.

His nine children were closely supervised. Matthew – the 'Arnold' of this book – was his first son, born in 1822. Mary Arnold was mostly occupied in caring for her family, and when Arnold was two years old she consulted a Harley Street doctor about weakness in his legs that may have been caused by rickets. This led to his wearing leg-irons for two years, though these did not prevent his lasting clumsiness. At Rugby, Mary's mothering extended to a pupil who was nearly four years older than Arnold, Arthur Hugh Clough. Clough was frequently taken into the family home and later became Arnold's close friend, and a poet; by all accounts, his scrupulousness was not lessened by the Arnolds' taxing regime.

Resistance to established interests was central to Dr Arnold's reforming modernity and to his role in one of the major controversies of the nineteenth century, over the relationship between the Church and the state. Here he led 'Broad Church' opposition to a group of anti-liberal clerics who were based in Oxford, the Tractarians. This high Church group – who included Newman – sought to reform society through the revival of religious faith. To combat the Movement's conservative approach to social reform, Dr. Arnold wrote in periodical journals, newspapers and pamphlets. His most passionate outburst followed his discovery of the machinations of the Oxford men against a Broad Church appointee at the university. With the publication of his essay on 'The Oxford Malignants and Dr Hampden', in the *Edinburgh Review*, his high public profile gathered notoriety. After detailed exposure of the Tractarian politics, this essay rails against Tractarian fanaticism. Arnold's habit of engaging in public controversy follows this paternal model, though his use of tact at times contrasts with his father's bluntness.

Arnold's sense of self was formed in this varied, warm yet strenuous and closely monitored life. As a defence against his parents' control, he developed a lack of seriousness. At just seven he produced grim 'Pimgrim', for instance, in a poorly received imitation of *Pilgrim's Progress*. Any provocation in the playful imitation of one of his father's favourite books, perhaps unconscious, was heightened by its dedication to 'His Holiness Lord Man'. His self-assertiveness increasingly took the form of facetiousness against Dr Arnold's high seriousness. Yet he became sensitive to oppression, apparently in reaction to his father's forcefulness and his own lameness. Evidence for this appears in his later protests against subordination. Signs of personal oppression can be discerned in his early essay 'Democracy' (1861), when it asserts that 'Life consists, say the philosophers, in the effort to *affirm one's own essence*; meaning by this, to develop one's own existence fully and freely, to have ample light and air, to be neither cramped nor overshadowed' (II: 7). This passage

11

suggests suffering in words that imply leg-irons and lack of recognition, 'cramped' and 'overshadowed'. As this writing invokes a human psychology as real and shared as human physiology, social and political disadvantage are seen to function like a poor physical frame in preventing self-realization.

This apparent identification with the oppressed suggests Arnold's own imaginative investment in greater equality. To glance ahead again for a moment, in his 1853 poem, 'Sohrab and Rustum', paternal overshadowing even seems to prompt his loose identification with the working-class, as a father's relationship with his son is figured in a curious simile:

> As some rich woman, on a winter's morn,
> Eyes through her silken curtains the poor drudge
> Who with numb blackened fingers makes her fire.
> ...so Rustum eyed
> The unknown adventurous youth

(P 302, l. 308-9).

This simile's fancifulness discountenances much weighting of Arnold's identification with this 'drudge', yet the poem is based on the failure of a father and a son to recognize each other as such, and, most obviously, the class difference of the 'drudge' suggests Dr Arnold's misrecognition of his own 'adventurous youth'.

A sense of injustice was not lessened by Arnold's two years away from home at a preparatory school from the age of eight, and a further year away at Winchester public school before he joined Rugby in 1837; in between the boarding schools he was tutored at home. He was often a reluctant pupil. Dr Arnold had introduced modern languages, mathematics and history at Rugby, but classical texts nonetheless dominated his son's education, with repeated demands for translation and exercises in grammar and paraphrase. The lessons required attention to the sounds, associations and contexts of words, and Arnold's poetic and journalistic abilities would draw on this schooling in the use of words and their effects.


## OXFORD AND LONDON

In 1841, in the footsteps of Clough, Arnold became an undergraduate at Oxford University, at Balliol College. His first term coincided with his father's inaugural lecture, following his appointment as Regius Professor of Modern History. A classical education, and Aristotle especially, still dominated the Oxford syllabus. As Arnold listened to his father's lecture, its combined subjective and objective approach introduced ideas of syllabus reform that only gained momentum at the end of the 1840s. An Idealist philosophical inheritance and Romanticism informed its emphasis on the inner life of a nation and the reform of History through new study of the peoples of post-classical times. The lecture was also indebted to the German historian who advocated scientific, empirical methods, Barthold Niebuhr: Modern History required scientific methods as well as organic nationalism. Dr Arnold's scientific interests further embraced German 'higher' criticism that led to Bible study in which he asked whether certain passages seemed like eye-witness accounts. His combination of subjective faith and objective reason were most clearly in tension as he investigated the gospels' veracity. Arnold's sensitivity to the effects of language seems grounded in his early experience of the discrediting of biblical words and, at the same time, their power to move audiences.

A legacy of reason and faith, or objectivity and subjectivity, informs most of Arnold's writing. He came to know public life from inside-out as he encountered, domestically, the conflict between reason, faith and feeling that marked the period, and when Dr Arnold died suddenly in the summer of 1842, he declared that his 'sole source of *information*' had gone (*L:* 5). His later elegy for his father, 'Rugby Chapel' (1867), labours the heavy sense of gloom that he had felt on the loss of his father's 'radiant vigour'. Dr Arnold's enthusiasm and excitement in modern life had entailed keeping up with European thought and at Rugby he had introduced modern subjects in advance of their study at Oxford. Yet inflexibility and impetuosity had limited his effectiveness. Even his devoted biographer, A.P. Stanley suggests how his forcefulness in expression inhibited his Oxford pupils. When Arnold enthuses over 'reason as the rock of refuge to this poor exaggerated, surexcited humanity' (1: 176), and demonstrates profound attachment to reason and sanity, it seems partly in reaction to Dr Arnold's 'surexcited' tendencies.

His father's calm antagonist, Newman, exerted a special

influence on Arnold. Relatively casually, Arnold had extricated himself from religious observance, and one of his letters parodies the Tractarians mercilessly (1: 64). Nonetheless he regularly attended Newman's riveting performances before an Oxford congregation. And although he disregarded the sermons' theology, it seems he realized through them, more than ever before, the poetry in religion and the force of style. Arnold's brother, Thomas, writes how 'the delicacy and refinement of his [Newman's] style were less cognisable to me than my brother, and the multiplied quotations from Scripture, introduced by "And again" – "And again"...confused and bewildered me'.[4] Arnold especially valued Newman's lucidity, which derived partly from these simple conjunctions, repetition, effective quotation and lists, and the use of scenic representation that worked on his hearers' emotions. His later use of these devices indicates Newman's influence on his own literary style in addition to his well-documented intellectual importance.

At Oxford in the 1840s much of his time was spent in discussing poetry with Clough and other friends and acquaintances. After he won the Newdigate Prize for his poem 'Cromwell', in 1843, his own occasional poetry writing became more regular. He also read widely, and this heightened the attachment to reason that had come from his classical schooling. The classical foundation of his scientific leaning to observation was underlined later when he described Aristotle as the 'scientific side' of the Greek genius (6: 21). His wide reading included modern and classical philosophers – Immanuel Kant, George Hegel, John Locke, Plato, the Stoics and the Epicureans. He also read Romantic authors, with particular enthusiasm for the many-sided German writer, J.W. von Goethe, and the French novelist, George Sand. In life, he experimented in his pose of an aesthete, which continued after Oxford. Like his facetiousness, this pose that kept others at a distance was both defensive and self-assertive.

In the 1830s Dr Arnold's methods had started to produce an identifiable new elite that was composed of pupils who went from Rugby to Oxford – especially Balliol – then on to public service. After briefly teaching at Rugby, and a fellowship at Oriel, Arnold went on from Oxford to work in London in 1847, as private secretary to Lord Lansdowne, Lord President of the

Council in the liberal Cabinet of Lord John Russell. It might seem that Arnold was following a pattern of public service that his father had prescribed, but the undemanding nature of the work enabled him to pursue his poetry writing. He was also able to explore the social power of language and literature through associationist psychology and theological and philological studies at London University where he was familiar with the work of F.D. Maurice and J.A. Scott. Scott was the Professor of English at University College from 1848. In stressing the role of literature in securing an intellectual deliverance from the confusion of modern society, Arnold's later inaugural lecture as Oxford Professor of Poetry seems to echo the theme of Scott's inaugural lecture in 1848, the role of literature in shaping national consciousness.[5] Both Scott and Maurice were preoccupied with the emotional power of literature and language.

Arnold's work also enabled him to travel to the Continent, where a trip to Paris during the Revolution of 1848 demonstrated literature's power in practice in shaping national life. For the political upheaval displayed the force of popular culture – how, 'amongst a *people* of readers the litterature [sic] is a greater engine than the philosophy', and 'Seditious songs have nourished the F[rench] people much more than the Socialist: philosophers: though they may formulize their wants through the mouths of these' (1: 92). Journalism's specific strength emerges here as an agent of *praxis* – that is, the union of thought and action – as it supplies 'applied ideas' for readers (1: 92). We have glimpsed how Arnold's writing indirectly identifies with oppression; in this March letter he seems positively drawn towards the subversive 'people' as they arouse his anti-authoritarian feelings. Yet these letters fluctuate in their attitudes almost daily, and another letter that derogatorily refers to the 'cock-and-bull excitement of common men' hopes that the aristocracy will continue (1: 86).

Arnold recounts his experience of revolution in one of his many letters to Clough between 1845 and 1853. His correspondence and private jottings that were written during his employment with Lansdowne demonstrate the extent of his questioning from his mid-twenties. Not only had he been introduced to the century's intellectual, literary, religious and political upheavals from his cradle, he had been drilled to question what he saw and believed. As we will see shortly, the themes in his writing – from the burden of the past to the difficulties of knowledge, modern poetry, language and his inner self – reflect this range and they run across all his late-1840s writing. To glance ahead at this private writing for a moment, Arnold tells Clough of his ideas and anxieties freely, and he dramatises how he needs him – 'Adieu and love me...I have a real craving to see you again' (1: 236): in their intimacy, his letters come nearer to love than any of his love poetry. Yet Arnold's letters – which are far more numerous than Clough's letters to Arnold – show how their differences grew and by 1853 Arnold's letters had become cool. At mid-century, Clough appears to him a poet whose intensity is unsuited to 'the sensuousness of poetry' and he admonishes, 'consider whether you attain the beautiful' (1: 131). For Arnold here the 'sensuousness of poetry' requires arranging and delineating '*objects*' through their surfaces, in 'airy and rapidly moving life', to make aesthetically pleasing poems where broad description, narrative and the sound of verbal arrangements are important. He proposes how, in Clough's case, this creation of works of art is precluded by the essence-seeking, inward character of thought – 'trying to go into & to the bottom of an object' (1: 131). To Clough, on the other hand, Arnold's poetry seems over-educated and unduly resistant to political action.[6]

Experiences of social displacement, political conflict and sexual attraction were also related to Arnold's movement from poetry to worldly concerns. His awkwardness over his erratic performance in Lansdowne's aristocratic milieu can be seen in a note where he observes how 'the nerves are wrong, the manners full of blunder and despicability' (*Y*: 84). At its outset, Clough had been disparaging about this slight employment that was at odds with Arnold's seriousness: as Arnold recoils from his own social ineptitude we glimpse how his liability to 'blunder' heightened the incongruity of holding a position that was something of a sinecure and which was, besides, linked to reactionary interests. When he is not caught up in the excitement of high life and parroting 'my man', Lansdowne, or despising himself, he is prone to scorn those he mixes with – 'the presence of a dead barren negative callosity' (*Y*: 168), for instance. As a Whig, Lansdowne was liberal in many of his views. But he was a *laissez-faire* liberal who resisted State expenditure, and he was a large land-holder in Ireland. His hostility to State action to prevent deaths in the Irish famine of 1847, and his callous estimate of a million deaths, apparently lie behind Arnold's poem, 'Horatian Echo' (1847), that reviles 'ye imbeciles in present power / Doomed, pompous and absurd!' (*P*: 59, l: 12). Nonetheless, this poem (which was unpublished until 1887) feebly urges avoidance of political life.

The anxieties that were directly related to Arnold's work with Lansdowne were heightened by the social and political upheavals of 1848. Additionally, on a trip to Switzerland in September that year he apparently first encountered the woman who would become the basis of his conflicted sequence of poems to 'Marguerite'. His contact with her seems to have been slight and scholars have argued over her identity.[7] The exposure that came with the publication of his first volume, *The Strayed Reveller and Other Poems*, in February 1849, brought further acute self-assessment. In the autumn of 1849 he finally gave up his love interest in 'Marguerite' and began writing the poems that told of this obscure relationship.

His introspection in the late 1840s contributed to the change in his second volume of poetry and to his transition to criticism. As he neared his thirtieth birthday, his life also changed outwardly in his courtship of Frances Lucy Wightman, a judge's daughter and a Tory. They were married in the summer of 1851, after Arnold's appointment as a schools inspector. Their first child was born in July 1852, and it was in October that year that his second volume, *Empedocles on Etna and Other Poems*, was published. His *Poems: a New Edition* followed very quickly, in November 1853, a month after his second child was born. His educational work entailed travel across the country. The 'Preface' to the *Poems: a New Edition* issued from this busy domestic and professional life.

## POETRY, LETTERS, NOTES

Arnold's relatively small poetic output consists of one hundred and thirty published poems that make up one volume; his criticism consists of eleven volumes of prose. In his lifetime, his importance as a poet was generally seen to rest on fewer than a dozen poems that were mostly written between 1849 and 1853. These poems delineate feelings of disunity so evocatively that Arnold is primarily viewed as a lyric poet now. Yet from such poems he achieves exemplary importance through producing enduring pictures of modernity and selfhood. These centre on self-consciousness and separation from the world, under the weight of the representations that overlay it. Privately, he writes of how life is dimmed in the stories we tell: 'Life is before the narration of life. Narrative is but the pal'd and waning shadow of fact' (Y: 165). As he construes his predicament in terms of such veiled existence, language assumes philosophical importance as the foundational form of publicity and estrangement. His typical protagonist is, moreover, historically cut off – 'wandering between two worlds' and lacking in wholeness: internally, and in the world around him, he is subject to division. Like his 1853 protagonist, Empedocles, he is confronted with the fact that 'To tunes we did not call our being must keep chime' (P: 173, l: 196). At the worst – like Empedocles – he is overcome by all that surrounds him, and no clear way ahead is discernible. At the best, as in 'The Scholar Gypsy', he tells of a free and whole existence, but this belongs in the past, away from 'the infection of our mental strife' (P: 368, l: 222). The clearest testimony to Arnold's representative importance is the continuing wide circulation of one lyrical poem of modern disconnection above all, 'Dover Beach'.

His poetic reputation rose slowly and unsteadily in his lifetime. The critic J.C. Shairp echoed other critics in his response to *Empedocles on Etna* when he protested how Arnold's poetry 'takes the life from out things' and 'disowns man's natural feelings' (CHP: 11). While Arnold's reputation as a poet reached a height from the late 1860s, it has always involved elements of repudiation and qualification that replicate the tenor of his poems. An editor of criticism on his poetry summarises how the Victorians found him 'a puzzling poet in an admittedly "transitional" age' (CHP: 5). A century later, 'readers still find his poetry limited in passion, flawed in technique, even slender in appeal' (CHP: 6). These indications of deficiency and even abjection in Arnold's poetry point towards its honesty and power, in publicizing a version of modern life that goes against the grain of liberal optimism. An anthology of Victorian writing conjures a somewhat abject figure who is marked by a 'lack of poetic exuberance, a failure in the vitality of his language', yet Arnold's presence here is considerable and this seems right for his poems have unusual verisimilitude that has to do with their restraint.[8] Since the 1980s, significant readings have explored their basis in his related allegiances – to scientific and poetic language in David Riede's study, *Matthew Arnold and The Betrayal of Language*, and to objectivity and subjectivity in Isobel Armstrong's book, *Victorian Poetry*. These analyses of a double Arnold point to conflicts in early nineteenth-century culture that we have glanced at in his upbringing, and they correspond with his own analysis in 1869 where he attributes his poems' representative character to their 'applied fusion' of 'poetic sentiment' and 'intellectual vigour' (3: 347).

Few poems in the *Strayed Reveller* are outwardly occupied by modern life, however, except in their attempt to correct certain beliefs – especially Romantic beliefs. Over his lifetime, Arnold writes about all the best known Romantic poets – Percy Bysshe Shelley, Lord Byron, Samuel Taylor Coleridge, William Wordsworth and John Keats. These writers' Romanticism differs greatly yet they share values that centre on the importance of the individual, self-expression, feelings, creativity, imagination and nature. Arnold's long didactic poem, 'Resignation' (1843-8), stands out in its revision of Romanticism, and especially the optimistic belief in nature, or naturalism, that was associated with Wordsworth at one time.

It is important here as it demonstrates how an argument about the importance of facts and the observable world is at stake in commitment to a wide perspective, for such insistence on an inclusive, general view is typical of Arnold's later criticism. The poem rewrites Wordsworth's 'Tintern Abbey', most obviously by addressing the speaker's sister and revisiting old walking country. Its support of scientific detachment is maintained stylistically in long descriptions. Wordsworthian nature is a living organism, in which the boundaries between different objects are blurred and they take on living form. Arnold's descriptions proceed factually, by naming and listing discrete natural features. One list moves up along 'the valley's western boundary', through the gate and valley-pastures, past the 'rude stone bridge' and 'western ridge', 'dark upland farms ... – cool farms, with open-lying stores' (*P*: 91, from l: 47). The factual ground that this covers bears out the poet-speaker's message, '*Not deep the poet sees, but wide*' (*P*: 97, l: 214).

At a key point, the speaker distinguishes himself from the poet's inspiration and 'rapt security' and claims that his detachment enables proper observation:

> And though fate grudge to thee and me
> The poet's rapt security,
> Yet they, believe me, who await
> No gifts from chance, have conquered fate.
> They, winning room to see and hear,
> And to men's business not too near,
> Through clouds of individual strife
> Draw homeward to the general life.

> (*P*: 99, l. 245–52)

The idea of 'winning room to see and hear', or necessary distance, and the 'general life', add to a picture of objective realism that entails broad vision, plain diction, and careful itemisation. Rather than finding joy in nature straightforwardly, the speaker highlights his awareness of his wish to find stoicism in nature:

> The solemn hills around us spread,
> This strange stream which falls incessantly,
> The strange-scrawled rocks, the lonely sky,
> If I might lend their life a voice,
> Seem to bear rather than rejoice.

> (*P*: 100, l. 266–70)

These lines have been read in terms of duty – what the speaker 'must scrupulously point out'.[9] Yet they suggest some pleasure in contemplating nature's inscrutability and also quite righteous pleasure in accuracy – how the speaker is *inclined* to see a particular message about endurance in nature, *and* that he knows that this reading is without warrant. The word 'seems' advertises the likely error in deducing anything from the hills, stream, rocks, sky. Specific words with romantic associations – like 'strange-scrawled rocks' – underline how this approach differs from romantic poets who read messages from nature (the poem's editors see echoes of Wordsworth's 'There was a boy...' here, and Shelley's 'Mont Blanc' is another possible allusion: *P*:

99, n. 265–8). 'Resignation' thus illustrates Arnold's sceptical attitude to what he sees as Romantic myths of creativity and nature.

However his argument with Romanticism was ambivalent. In poems that dramatise different kinds of self in writing on classical subjects, his attraction to sensual modes and extreme affective states is striking. In the atmospheric 'New Sirens' (1846–7), for instance, two forms of emotional disengagement are opposed, in an *'alternation* of ennui [languor] and excitement' that Arnold associates with modernity (*P*: 49). Another atmospheric poem, 'The Forsaken Merman', was the most liked by reviewers of *The Strayed Reveller* – and also by the twentieth-century poet, Sylvia Plath. Based on a fairy-tale, it moves between sensual existence in underwater caverns and mechanical labour on the high ground of a 'white-walled town' (*P*:102, l: 25). The fantastic marine world appears in much-quoted lines that describe the merman's abode:

> Where the sea-beasts, ranged all round,
> Feed in the ooze of the pasture-ground;
> Where the sea-snakes coil and twine,
> Dry their mail and bask in the brine.
> Where great white whales come sailing by,
> Sail and sail, with unshut eye....

(P:102, l: 35–44)

The evocation of sensuality beneath the 'surf' and 'swell' rests on a kind of naming where creatures do what they do slowly, in plain verbs. As well as the end-rhymes, plain words across just a few lines are joined in homophony – 'weed', 'feed', 'mail', 'whales' – so that mere verbal arrangement achieves strong poetic effects aurally. This illustrates Arnold's idea of 'the sensuousness of poetry' very well.

This forceful poem was untypical, and the quotations that we have seen illustrate only a little of the variety in the 1849 volume. This variety, and many distant, classical and exotic subjects ('The Sick King in Bokhara' and 'Fragment of an "Antigone"', for example) make it seem that Arnold's poems lack a strong centre. Within them, poetic individuality is unorthodoxly manifest in virtuosity, ingenuity, argument, accuracy. The few readers of his first volume were disturbed by its lack of force and clear purpose. *Blackwood's Magazine's* bluff demand, 'What would our friend be at?' (*CHP*: 55), voiced a bafflement that appeared in more liberal reviews also.

Arnold's intense preoccupation with his own identity and purpose in the months that surrounded this first publication appears in his volatile 'dialogue of the mind with itself' in his letters and private notes that suggest a philosopher in the making. One 'dialogue' displays the difficulty of forming opinions: 'So and so gives an opinion – how did he form it – penetrate yourself with the slight accidental way in wch ABC & D form & state opinions' (*Y*: 171). Reason and feeling are visibly in conflict as an entry that favours reason is followed by another in which 'the service of reason is freezing to feeling' (*Y*: 160). Shifting connotations of the 'people' display Arnold's instability further and these are especially important since his later critical purpose can be mapped in terms of the shifting states of 'people'.

His championship of 'a *people* of readers' who read 'litterature' as opposed to philosophy refers to people on the streets in 1848, and all those who challenge authority (1: 92). Here he apparently writes 'a people' emotionally and unthinkingly, with Romantic and political associations with revolution and nationalism. This positive charge of the word 'people' is strengthened by its importance in the Bible, which tells of how 'the people that walked in darkness have seen a great light' (*King James Bible*, Isaiah 9:2). But on one occasion, when he has been reading George Sand, 'a people' is ruthlessly questioned as a term: 'For my soul I cannot *understand* this violent praise of the people. I praise a fagot whereof the several twigs are nought: but a *people*?' (1: 103). As scepticism prevails, 'a people' seems a phantom: to whom does it refer? is this collectivity based on popular, or national, belonging – and how? Arnold's linguistic hesitation over 'a people' and his epistemological confusion over the validity of reason and the senses are closely intertwined. Implicitly, his own identity is at issue – is *he* someone who uses that name, *people*? how are *people* distinct from him? His first reference to publicity, in 1849 or 1850, suggests its distorting effect: too much 'labouring after expression and publicity' precludes a 'feeling of the whole' (*Y*: 171). His hesitations over 'a people' suggest that 'a feeling of the whole' may in some cases not have a valid verbal equivalent since it *is only* a feeling. 'Common men' and the 'masses' appear in his 1848 letters as 'people' in an unruly and inchoate form. His critical imagination will centre on securing commonality so that the disparate strands of people are smoothed into a uniform public.

His anxiety at mid-century centres on such problems with language and the way that his public utterance exposes his divided self and his poetry's lack of unity. His letters to Clough address such inadequacies – often by criticizing such faults in Clough – and they suggest how he was starting to find his own 'way' through his understanding of the role of Ideas, *praxis* and practical reason. So he proposes that poets 'must begin with an Idea of the world in order not to be prevailed over by the world's multitudinousness' (1: 128). This capitalized 'Idea' suggests Coleridge's sense of that word, 'that conception of a thing, which is not abstracted from any particular state, form or mode, in which the thing may happen to exist at this or that time . . . but which is driven by knowledge of its *ultimate aim*'.[10] This 'Idea' that poets need relates to what exists now *and* its purposeful, or teleological, development – hence their writing does not need to correspond to things as they are. Moreover this 'Idea' brings unity and strength through its ability to shape material. The importance of creating works of art through Ideas appears as Arnold objects to 'using poetry as a vehicle for thinking aloud, instead of *making* anything' (1: 141).

Yet Arnold observes 'how deeply *unpoetical* the age and all one's surroundings are' (1: 131), and he admits that he may give up his attempt to write poetry. In another letter to Clough, in September 1849, he moves towards the world further and towards greater integration as he invokes *praxis*, the term that denotes rational *action*:

> What I must tell you is that I have never yet succeeded in any one great occasion in consciously mastering myself: I can go thro: the imaginary process of mastering myself & see the whole affair as it would then stand, but at the critical point I am too apt to hoist up the mainsail to the wind and let her drive. . . . I find that with me a clear almost palpable intuition (damn the logical senses of the word) is necessary before I get into praxis: unlike many people who set to work at their duty, self-denial &c. like furies in the dark hoping to be gradually illuminated as they persist in this course. Who also perhaps may be

sheep but not of my fold, whose one natural craving is not for profound thoughts, mighty spiritual workings &c. &c. but a distinct seeing of my way as far as my own nature is concerned. (1: 156)

Apparent weakness here becomes a source of strength as Arnold relaxes from 'consciously mastering myself'. The context of the passage makes it likely that it refers to his difficulties in writing, and the editor of the *Letters*, Cecil Lang, takes it this way (1: xxiii). The external routes of right conduct and duty, intellect and 'mighty spiritual workings &c. &c.' are here all relegated when it comes to ascertaining Arnold's own practice, or 'praxis' (Cecil Lang points out that the word was long mistaken for 'prayer'). As Arnold detaches himself from these standard routes of a Protestant sensibility, his *praxis* purportedly derives from an intuitive, independent process based on his senses ('almost palpable', 'seeing of my own way').

Aptly, then, he earlier appears 'snuffing for a moral atmo-sphere to respire in' (1: 155). In this dog-like resistance to logic and asceticism, his 'own nature' first appears in this letter as he seeks an 'atmosphere' to breathe. Such sensory activity is related to Aristotle when his *Ethics* is quoted from later in the letter. Where this appears, Arnold enjoins: 'Let us be neither fanatics or yet chalf [sic] blown by the wind' but let us be *as the man of practical wisdom would define it, and not as any one else would define it* ' [my italics] (1: 156). Arnold actually quotes from the Greek, which uses the word *phronesis* – a word that also translates as practical reason, practical sense, prudence and common sense. In the *Ethics*, the quality is illustrated by Pericles and those who 'can envisage what is good for themselves and for people in general: we consider that this quality belongs to those who understand the management of households and nations'.[11] As one mode of practical reason, or *phronesis*, when it seeks the way ahead, 'snuffing' requires sign-reading or semiotic skill since it silently picks up clues. Leaning on *mores* or how things are done, it points to 'my way' in practice, making it no dry rule-book affair that is found through 'profound thoughts' but instead something that is scented out. This affirms a kind of embedded thought in atmosphere: from this 'snuffing' one can sift a direction, or an idea, with *praxis* working backwards from practice. Freedom, epistemology and materialism are all at stake in the odd expression – an early index of Arnold's empirical, anti-metaphysical course.

This letter's emphasis on the senses and experience corresponds with his other private writing. The account of *praxis* suggests how his action in writing poetry now follows from a firmer grasp or 'intuition' that provides a central Idea. Later, his criticism appears similarly structured by a central idea, of modernity – from which more customary associations of *praxis* with *political* action develop. Immediately, in 1849, Arnold started to produce bolder poems – as in the Marguerite sequence – apparently on the strength of his new understanding. His poems from 1849 to 1852 paint a broad picture of the loss of traditional authorities in the continuing upheaval since the French Revolution, science's growing importance and the discrediting of Christianity especially. The recurrence of the verb 'seems' in his poetry is one of the clearest if smallest indices of the many-fronted upheaval. Several poems are now grounded in present identifiable locations – 'Calais Sands', for instance, and Dover, looking onto a *beach*. We will look at three poems that in different ways bear on his later publicist identity, 'The Buried Life', 'Dover Beach' and 'Stanzas from the Grande Chartreuse'.

In 'The Buried Life' (1849-52) the speaker's feeling of not being centred is induced in the presence of a lover, whose 'inmost soul' (*P*: 289, 1: 111) he professes interest in. His further appearances, in public, in 'the world's most crowded streets', lead to a yearning that seems created by distraction:

> But often, in the world's most crowded streets,
> But often, in the din of strife,
> There rises an unspeakable desire
> After the knowledge of our buried life;
> A thirst to spend our fire and restless force
> In tracking out our own true, original course;
>
> A longing to inquire
> Into the mystery of this heart which beats
> So wild, so deep in us – to know
> Whence our lives come and whence they go.

(P: 289, 1: 45–54)

Through the correspondence between the 'crowded streets' and the 'din of strife', on the one hand, and his 'unspeakable' desire and 'wild' heart within, the speaker's sense of his own division is related to his distance from others. Namelessness and 'strife' mark both inner and outer worlds and they form the basis of the speaker's indirect identification with the crowd.[12] As he continues to complain of his lack of 'skill to utter one of all / The nameless feelings that course through our breast' (P: 290, 1: 61–2), his difficulty with his own public utterance, which seems like a bad performance, is paralleled by his difficulty in accessing public presence at all. The 'nameless feelings' attest to the difficulty in translating a 'feeling of the whole' into language (Y: 172). As the speaker's inner life is linked with the crowd their fortunes appear tied and we may glimpse how Arnold's working life will be bound up in the project of making others more articulate and speaking to the general public.

In an especially resonant passage the speaker appears at one with himself and a lover:

> Only – but this is rare – ...
> When our world-deafened ear
> Is by the tones of a loved voice caressed –
> A bolt is shot back somewhere in our breast,
> And a lost pulse of feeling stirs again.
> The eye sinks inward, and the heart lies plain,
> And what we mean, we say, and what we would, we know...
>
> (P: 291, 1: 77–87)

The arresting effect of these lines is tied to the startling 'bolt' and the way that 'the eye sinks inward'. Most blatantly in this uncouth, sinking eye (perhaps the mouth falls open too?), the passage manifests an intense desire for words to refer to the whole of experience; and also, taxingly, for words to say what 'we' mean, transparently, and not say something else. Yet the eye that 'sinks inward' loses sight, much as the ear in the crowd becomes deaf: the correspondence between private and public experience here underlines a fantasy of a generalized sociality in which all is admissible but is then quite indistinguishable. The usual fixture of a bolt on an outside door moreover suggests the entry of people on the 'crowded streets' when it is 'shot back', as if under pressure. The undoing of this incongruous bolt further suggests the imaginative appeal of the dissolution of indivi-duality for Arnold, as a perverse form of wholeness in which individuality is forfeited in the larger identity of a crowd. This poem seems indeed sprung on ambivalence about acquiring the skill to name things and, on the contrary, abandoning distinctions.

The lyrical power of 'Dover Beach' (1851) has to do with the way that private experience is reconfigured in public language. In its representation of psychic displacement, the poem shifts from a bedroom in a love scene in the English port to the ancient Aegean, and then to 'the world, which seems / to lie before us like a land of dreams' (*P*: 256, 1: 30–1) – a hollow echo of *Paradise Lost*, the epic poem by the seventeenth-century poet, John Milton. The fortunes of 'a thought' epitomize the permeability of boundaries, where private sensation 'picks up' spiritual and cultural loss. Like pebbles on this shore, 'which the waves draw back, and fling, / At their return, up the high strand' (*P*: 255, 1: 10–11), the thought of 'The Sea of Faith' is 'found' in the sound of the sea:

> ...we
> Find also in the sound a thought,
> Hearing it by this distant northern sea.
>
> The Sea of Faith
> Was once, too, at the full, and round earth's shore
> Lay like the folds of a bright girdle furled.
> But now I only hear
> Its melancholy, long, withdrawing roar,
> Retreating, to the breath
> Of the night-wind, down the vast edges drear
> And naked shingles of the world.
>
> (*P*: 255–6, 1: 18–28)

In many ways this poem's abandoned, confused cultural scene *is* Arnold's negative version of modernity. The decline in faith occupies most attention; the 'glimmering' of the Dover cliffs and the 'grating of pebbles' suggest the erosion of the shoreline and the weakness of nature according to evolutionary science, besides a failing England. A little earlier, the 'French coast', where 'the light / Gleams and is gone' (*P*: 254, 1: 3–4), conjures political upheaval from the French Revolution. A reference to the ancient Greek dramatist, Sophocles, and echoes of a Greek historian, Thucydides, complete the glancing anticipation of Arnold's critical interests in religion, science, Romanticism,

27

classical literature, national identity and the modern state. The above stanza duly conveys a prolonged, broadly-based retreat. This terminates abruptly with the stark long 'a' and disparity of scale in 'naked shingles of the world'. To see 'shingles' as 'naked' is somewhat forced – like the 'naked' piano legs that some Victorians had to cover – and this poem has elements of posturing (in the 'bright girdle' also) as it tries to make the outer world conform to inner feeling. Yet herein lies the uncomfortable naturalistic strength of Arnold's poetry, which does not gloss the awkwardness of existence where authority is lacking and authenticity is fraught.

In 'Stanzas from the Grande Chartreuse' (1851–55) the contemporary world comes more sharply into focus. Strictly speaking, the poem falls outside this discussion. Though most of it seems to have been written in 1852, it was not completed until after 1853. But the addition of a stanza that alludes to current affairs after 1853 importantly underlines how Arnold was turning from his general ideas about the world to forces that swayed English society. The poem is best known for its summary of the condition that his poems describe in general, of 'Wandering between two worlds' (*P*: 305, l: 85). The 'wandering' immediately refers to the limbo of existing between two historical worlds, 'one dead, / The other powerless to be born' (*P*: 305, l: 85–6): so far, it echoes 'Dover Beach' and many other poems. Yet 'Grande Chartreuse' offers a coda to these, as it elaborates the present historical middle ground, in the form of the Crimean War in which England was engaged at mid-century. Here it is English society itself that is seen in terms of opposition, between the world of 'Action and pleasure' and that of those whose 'bent was taken long ago' – like the poet-speaker (*P*: 311, l: 194, 198). The ascendancy of worldly forces is underlined in a stanza that hails

> with awe
> The exulting thunder of your race;
> You give the universe your law,
> You triumph over time and space!'

> (*P*: 309, l: 162–6)

The 'thunder of your race' apparently alludes to the *Times* newspaper, which became known as 'The Thunderer' for its loud opposition to the conduct of the War under the editor, W.T. Delane. The triumphal personification of this newspaper suggests a new godhead that usurps the functions of Government. The 'thunder' was based on the paper's exposure of inefficiency in the administration of the army, which was close to Arnold's own work as a civil servant. To the 'wandering' between past, present and future in the poem is hence added the movement between two cultural groups in English society, as we see the marginal poet-speaker wondering about journalism's effectiveness in apparent envy. His melancholy and marginality seem intensified through the exultation of the martial and journalistic interests that the paper represents, and its ability to uncover blunders.[13] For T.S. Eliot, this poem marks 'a moment of historic doubt, voiced by its most representative mind, a moment that has passed' (see *P:* 302), yet the marginality of artists continues. Arnold's terms, of 'wandering' and 'worlds', are more spatial than historical, and 'wandering between two worlds' has continuing resonance in relation to cultural displacement.

These three poems suggest Arnold's sense of powerlessness as well as his social awareness and attraction to public life. 'The Buried Life' indicates the appeal of 'the many' who are beyond the pale of respectable society; 'Stanzas from the Grande Chartreuse' registers the political power of the press, and a newspaper's plain, high style. In this it demonstrates Arnold's commitment to plain language in the 1850s. We have seen examples of his own poetic plainness. His 1840s' correspondence advocates plain language in the face of the 'multitude of new thoughts and feelings a modern has to deal with' (1: 78), and he would later uphold the plain, grand style of classical writers. Less abstract considerations of audience and communication appear in 1852 when he assigns 'great plainness of speech' to a 'mature ... age of the world': modern poetry has 'an immense task to perform ... it must not lose itself in parts and episodes and ornamental work, but must press forwards to the whole' (1: 245–6). The framing of 'exquisite bits' as decadent, and the 'immense task', point towards the 'whole' people in modern society, and it increasingly seems that Arnold is going to withdraw from this 'immense task', or else reinterpret it as a critical programme. He was acutely conscious of an unformed whole or 'mass' three months after he took up school work:

> The world tends to become more comfortable for the mass, and more uncomfortable for those of any natural gift or distinction – and it is as well perhaps that it should be so – for hitherto the gifted have astonished and delighted the world, but not trained or imagined it or in any real way changed it – and the world might do worse than dismiss too high pretensions, and settle down on what it can see and handle and appreciate. (1: 233)

In this movement from a privileged point of view to that of the less fortunate, a liberalism that stresses self-creation gives way to a more practical, social kind. The social cost of art is explicitly at issue, as artistic creativity is set against creativity that brings 'real' change. Far from being an ascetic, duty-bound undertaking, as the vocabularies of art and management intermingle – 'trained . . . imagined . . . handle . . . appreciate' – this social type of creativity looks at least as rich as a pure type that astonishes and delights.

A weighted use of 'plain' in Arnold's first school report, in the same year, underlines the social appropriateness of plainness in modern society: in the schools that spread education, young pupil teachers 'often cannot paraphrase a *plain* passage of prose or poetry' (my italics, S: 19). Arnold's growing insistence on plain expression in particular reflected widespread anxieties that poetry was losing effectiveness as a modern form. His poetry's low sales (he indicates only fifty copies of his 1853 volume were sold) were not unusual for classically-educated poets: 'people much prefer *Vanity Fair* and *Bleak House*', Clough argued in an essay of 1853 on the growing preference for fiction over poetry. For Clough, like Arnold, it is axiomatic that poetry needs 'to be widely popular, to gain the ear of multitudes, to shake the hearts of men', but for Clough poets need to write on contemporary life: 'poetry should deal more than at present it usually does, with general wants, ordinary feelings, the obvious rather than the rare facts of human nature'.[14]

'Empedocles on Etna' (1849–52) presents an extreme case of the modern condition. Through its main protagonist, the eponymous ancient Greek philosopher, the poem conveys the futility of endless questioning and introspection when there are no foundational truths. As a representative 'modern', Empedocles sets out to see things as they are and is sceptical: the more he seeks, the less he finds – 'I read / In all things my own deadness' (*P*: 200, l: 321–2). In his despair before his suicide he is deaf to the arguments and music of the harpist, Callicles, that might restore him to equanimity. Callicles' music and words *say* nothing that can bring Empedocles round, Empedocles refuses to *know* anything that can affect his own predicament. Callicles' inability to affect Empedocles seems pre-ordained in that he, Callicles, has hitherto avoided unpleasant realities, such as the barren slopes of Etna. The eirenic lines of Callicles' final song, after Empedocles' suicide, foreground poetry's indifference to suffering. For when he turns his gaze from the unpleasant scene on Etna he lays poetry open to critique on realist, empirical grounds: 'Not here, O Apollo! Are haunts meet for thee' (*P*: 204, l: 421–2). In the ambiguity of this exclamation poetry's marginality and ineffectiveness are implied.

The 'Preface' advertises the exclusion of 'Empedocles' from the 1853 *Poems: A New Edition* on account of its failure to 'inspirit and rejoice the reader' (*P*: 655). Arnold's commitment to words' correspondence to reality was apparently now taking the form of requiring that knowledge of modern unhappiness should become more 'real' in poetry, in the sense that poetry should act on this knowledge to lessen unhappiness. He writes to Clough in November 1852 that poetry's destination is not simply other poets as he complains about one of his poems,

'what does it *do* for you? . . . at best [it] awakens a pleasing melancholy. But this is not what we want.

> The complaining millions of men
> Darken in labour and pain –

what they want is something to *animate* and *ennoble* them' (sic, 1: 282).

'Pleasing melancholy' appears a somewhat indecent luxury that is confined to those who are remote from 'labour and pain'. Verbs like 'infuse', 'rejoice' and 'inspirit', however, present poetry as a form of action that works at a distance through influence that may relieve the pain of 'millions'.

In this confused context, then, the 'Preface' protectively advances a poetry that will similarly 'infuse delight' and create 'the highest enjoyment' (*P*: 655). Its idealist, affective poetic contrasts markedly with the social realism that Clough and other poets sought. Poetry's effects on readers here include its ability to 'inspirit' its audience, the skills that it propagates, and the sense of perspective that it imparts. The 'Preface''s proposals are loosely threefold: poets should take great human actions for their subject; they should seek architectonic form, 'that power of execution, which creates, forms and constitutes' (P: 664); and they should keep to a plain, grand style. Classical writers are seen as exemplary in these respects. Their art is contrasted with the 'morbid' 'dialogue of the mind with itself' of modern writers, and the 'vivid and picturesque turns of expression' of Keats, that give a momentary 'thrill' (P: 665). Here – where it indirectly challenges contemporary 'sensational' poetry – the 'Preface' quite clearly responds to periodical debate about poetry's future. Yet despite this challenge, Arnold's emphatic rejection of the 'dialogue of the mind with itself' takes up a widespread sense that such 'dialogue' was injurious. In his public turnaround about this characteristic of his own poetry it seems his words about suffering become real to him – that he elects to abandon the tortuous path of self-preoccupation, to seek effectiveness in alleviating other suffering.

His elevation of the past, classical writers and poetry's ethical function for large modern audiences brought widespread criticism.[15] The 'Preface' acknowledges that 'the confusion of present times is great, the multitude of voices counselling different things bewildering' (P: 663); yet its treatment of poetry's relation to the public is relatively slight. The 'complaining millions of men' do not appear here. At several points the 'Preface' is explicitly addressed to other writers (for examples, P: 663); it ends by suggesting that it may be impossible to write poetry of a classical type now (P: 671). And when it projects poetic creation as a kind of pregnancy (P: 659–60) it points to creative work that occurs outside poetry: a midwife is suggested as well as a sculptor when the Greek poet is seen to proceed 'stroke by stroke' while he brings to light what lies hidden in 'memory, as a group of statuary, faintly seen, at the end of a long and dark vista' (P: 660). Moreover this essay indicates that many people have a simplistic picture of 'early Greek genius': 'What those who are familiar only with the great monuments of early Greek genius suppose are its exclusive characteristics have disappeared [by the time of Empedocles]' (*P*: 654). If Empedocles is not a suitable subject for poetry, audiences evidently need to know about him.

In such ways, the 'Preface' actually makes poetry appear a limited, insufficient literary form in modern society. This has positive implications, however, for it underlines the need for criticism to supplement poetry on social and intellectual grounds. As poetry is circumscribed by the need to uplift men emotionally, criticism becomes more necessary. Moreover, the uplifting kind of poetry that Arnold outlines here is at odds with his acute vision and contentiousness: the 'Preface' delineates a kind of poetry that it will be relatively easy for him to walk away from. The fluency of his first-person prose essay suggests how he has found a new public voice and purpose in criticism that prescribes what is to be done – though labouring to produce the art that brings the 'highest enjoyment' will not suffice for him.

# 2

## 'The Empire of Facts': Inspection, Lectures and Criticism Until 1862

*He who administers, governs, because he infixes his own mark and stamps his character on all public affairs as they pass through his hands* (II: 6–7)

When Arnold became a government school inspector in 1851 he joined the professional bureaucracy of a modernizing state. A classical education was widely thought to qualify men for this civil service employment by giving them the necessary detachment for their work, especially for factual analysis. And a detached, reflective attitude was welcomed by politicians since it kept the civil servants at a distance from politics. Arnold's brief was to produce 'general reports' and 'general observations', whereby he functioned at the general, detached level that he had valued in poetry. He could also develop his ideas in practice in varied educational assignments and writing. Here he moved from seeking wholeness in himself to seeking greater breadth and wholeness in pupils and teachers, and a national system of education.[1]

As educational provision became more subject to parliamentary control, civil servants were widely supposed to keep distant from political controversy and maintain professional neutrality. But schools were enmeshed in power relations and Arnold's ideas developed during his educational work so that by the 1860s he was no stranger in the world of party politics. His work then brought him into the political arena in ways that ranged from attendance at parliamentary debates to lobbying politicians and writing political criticism. His first writing in periodical

34

journals, in 1862, when he took on a propagandist role, was driven by the educational views that are elaborated in this chapter. His publicist activity in general arose from his belief in modern education through state intervention; his 1862 essay, 'The Twice-Revised Code', publicized his opposition to the plans of the Liberal Education Minister, Robert Lowe, for a system of 'payment by results' in elementary schools. This will be discussed in the next chapter since it bore importantly on his subsequent writing as a publicist.

His educational work was also important in the evolution of his views on order. For the ideas and methods that he urges in schools were a foundation for his ideas and writing about culture in *Culture and Anarchy*. Most obviously, the word 'culture' appears in his school reports with reference to an individual's mental cultivation and his or her development and integration of different faculties; so, in 1863, he writes of the 'rate of culture', and the greater 'positive culture' of 'Scotch students' (S: 107, 108). His thinking on this project of self-development, or humanization, was influenced by Newman and German 'higher' critics who included J.G. Herder and Willhelm von Humboldt; the word 'culture' appears mainly in this sense in this chapter which considers its practical import. Here pupils' emotional responses to literary texts and teachers, and financial recognition for the teachers, are all vital for good teaching. Arnold's ideas about pupils' needs in learning are followed through later in his publicist work where he imagines his audience in particular ways.

It is necessary to backtrack to 1851 as this chapter focuses first on Arnold's routine school work amidst an unprecedented proliferation of printed matter, before turning to his writing as a modern critic. At a time when publicity was newly important, Arnold was professionally required to spread knowledge of schools' performance by producing reports on the schools that he visited. The slight suspension of chronology when considering his ongoing school employment underlines the complex interrelationship of his different roles, even before his critical career got underway properly with his appointment as the Professor of Poetry at Oxford in 1857. He secured this Chair on the strength of the growing reputation of his early poetry. In his lectures he at once distanced himself from his public identification as a poet in his proposals about social transformation. His inaugural lecture, 'On the Modern Element in Literature', marked his public emergence as a critic as it abandoned the poetic topics that earlier Professors had lectured on, such as the nature of imagination. The classical features and poor reception of his long verse-drama that he produced at this time, 'Merope', underlined the distance between his role as a poet and a critic. Yet in his university work, as in schools, he pursued the preoccupations of his early poetry which centred on questions of modernity.

From 1857 to 1862, his first five-year term at Oxford established his own modern portfolio existence as a critic who spent most of his working days in his educational employment, while he continued to write poetry occasionally. At Oxford he was required to lecture three times a year and to undertake some official duties, such as judging poetry competitions. In 1859, his school work included membership of the Newcastle Commission on Popular Elementary Education, which brought six months visiting schools on the Continent before writing up his report. Through this travel, he also produced a political pamphlet. From thinking about his own fragmentation in his early poetry, he now moved between different kinds of public performance where his methods and thinking varied according to his different roles. The following account traces his emergence as a civil servant in education and then as a critic, and the adaptations and innovations that these roles entailed. Here modernity will be seen to mean a number of different but related things.

## SCHOOL INSPECTING

In his educational employment Arnold was at once practically engaged in creating a modern social order that was marked by a new inclusiveness. As a schools' inspector he supervised the provision of elementary education for children whose schooling was supported by public funds, who were unlikely to receive education without such funding. His first schools' report complained about the rare attendance of the children of the poor compared with the children of the middle classes. It registered explicitly the nation-building role of education in its opposition to the preservation of the Welsh language in schools: 'it must always be the desire of a Government to render its dominions, as far as possible, homogenous' (S: 13). And it observed how the study of English literature and composition would 'have the great social advantage of tending to bring them ['a number of young men'] into intellectual sympathy with the educated of the upper classes' (S: 20). The cultivation of emotional, moral and intellectual capacities was supposed to overcome class conflict by inducing a sense of shared human identity: as pupils became 'humanized' through such cultivation, they would tend to discount the material differences between social classes.

As Arnold seeks to displace the class conflicts of modern society through elementary schooling, it can seem that from the outset his idea of culture is opposed to political action. His educational work has thus contributed to oppositional accounts of *Culture and Society*, where the two terms are seen in conflict.[2] Yet the modern state is itself a political institution that encompasses central and local administration as well as the formal political organ, the Houses of Parliament, in which government is centred. As a civil servant, Arnold sought the extension of education through a centralized state, and his neglected political action centres on this commitment. Not only was the state a political body, its expansion was the object of controversial Parliamentary legislation at a time when much liberal political opinion was committed to free trade, limited government expenditure, efficiency and *laissez-faire* or non-intervention by the state.

Before he emerged as a political propagandist in 1862, Arnold's educational work demonstrated his dedication to an integrated modern state through education. In their book, *Culture and the State*, the American critics, David Lloyd and Paul Thomas, directly relate the dissolution of class consciousness through Arnoldian pedagogy to the state's disinterested stance, as pupils' experience of trusting the ethical adults in the classrooms prepares them for *being* represented in a democratic state.[3] Here we will see how Arnold advances the politically-charged goal of efficiency, as well as critical detachment and disinterest, in his role as a modern Inspector.

State support of schools had been introduced in 1833 in the provision of grants to the charitable religious foundations that provided education for the poor. The support had been strengthened in 1846 with the introduction of school inspectors to ensure that the grants were not mis-spent, though their inspection was then without legal enforcement. Arnold moved from working as Lansdowne's private secretary to working as one of these inspectors. When he joined this infant professional bureaucracy, the state had hesitantly embarked on the uncertain course of national education. His responsibility was the 'elementary schools' of the Dissenters – the Nonconformist Methodists and other Christian denominations outside the Church of England – in an area from Great Yarmouth on the east coast of England to most of Wales. At stages in the future his area became smaller, until it was centred on London; in 1871 he became a senior inspector, and in 1883, chief inspector. The schools offered a basic training for children up to the age of fourteen, and in his first year he inspected one hundred and twenty of these institutions.

The inspectors' work included carrying out oral and written tests on the pupils and the apprentice pupil-teachers. They then produced detailed information on individual schools and general reports. The reports were presented to the Education Committee of the Privy Council and published as parliamentary papers in the Houses of Parliament. The Education Committee largely operated autonomously, 'by rules of its own framing, embodied in various Minutes, the most important...provided an elaborate system of state encouragement and control in the training, certification, and payment of teachers' (Super, II: 348). One of the inspectors' main functions was to publicize good practice and new thinking, and in this respect their employment mimicked the work of the teachers that they inspected. Their considerable powers are reflected in this chapter's epigraph which suggests how Arnold felt empowered in executive work that seemed a form of government. While this might seem a fantasy of power on his part, the Education Committee's regulation of schools through successive 'Minutes' in fact bypassed parliamentary processes. From 1860, following the codification and new legal warrant of these regulations, adjustments to the 'Code' acquired the force of statute law annually merely through being laid before the House of Commons for a month, subject to amendment.

When the state support for 'public education' had been introduced in 1833, it had been just one of many reform measures through which different areas of civil life were brought under state regulation. This introduction of state aid reflected concerns about the subversive potential of 'the people'. These were mixed with a new conception of the state as *the representative* of the people of a nation, that nonetheless had responsibilities to *create* this people – a unifed, cohesive body, that is. We will see more of Arnold's own awareness of the French Revolution's ideological importance in instituting 'the people' as a political force, that he had shown in 1848, and his fundamental assumption that 'the masses of people.. are preparing to take a much more active part than formerly in controlling its destinies' (II: 15).

Still, his school reports more obviously respond to the proliferation of printed matter and an overload of information than anxieties about subversion. This textual proliferation was particularly evident in the huge growth of journalism from the 1840s to the 1860s, and in government reports that addressed the new social conditions of an industrial society. Henry Mayhew's series of articles on *London Labour and the London Poor* in the *Morning Chronicle* in 1849-50 clearly demonstrated the commercial appeal of related newspaper documentary investigation. The spectacle of mismanagement in reports of the Crimean War in the *Times* in 1854 was quite similarly both informative and sensational. Arnold's reference to the 'empire of facts' in his 1853 'Preface' to his *Poems* may allude to this new kind of sensational journalism in the main London daily papers as well as the fact-finding work of civil servants like himself. The importance of large readerships for newspapers increased after the abolition of the Stamp Duty on newspapers in 1855 when the English daily press began to develop on a new capital-intensive basis which was needed for technological innovations in production. The increased need for capital-expenditure was reflected in the greater role of advertisements in obtaining newspaper revenue.

With reference to more ephemeral publications than the journal from which he wrote, the sensation novelist, Wilkie

Collins, produced a famous article on 'The Unknown Public' in *Household Words* (21 August 1858). Collins' picture of an absence of discrimination in magazine production and consumption outlines a new 'sub-literate' readership who are able to read, but only in a passive way that seems mindless to Collins. Arnold's school reports share this anxiety about literacy in the face of the abundance of 'positive information', and the pupils' inability to steer through this material is a key component of his picture of modern confusion. Such concerns about new reading matter were complemented by some critics' adaptive approaches to established literary and pedagogical conventions. Most famously, the editor of the *National Review*, Walter Bagehot, announced in 1855 that ' "We must speak to the many so that they will listen – that they will like to listen – that they will understand....The multitude are impatient of system, desirous of brevity, puzzled by formality" '.[4] This was echoed in calls for the institutionalization of English studies, to provide a new form of study for the 'multitude' for whom long-established texts and methods in education were too remote. Arnold's reports similarly address the remoteness of learning for elementary school pupils.

The book collection of his general school reports which Francis Sandford published soon after Arnold's death omits his many tables and summaries of information that went into the school inspectors' parliamentary papers. This makes the factual, practical dimensions of Arnold's inspection less apparent and so his lucid reports may appear as simply a variation of his literary writing – a kind of literary realism. Yet material, practical details – from the distribution of furniture to data on several measures of ability – are central to the educational and national incoherence that his full reports portray in the 1850s, where efficiency is a key objective. In twenty-five pages of tabulated information in his first report, one school is for instance 'efficient on the whole' (Gainsborough), another 'will be more useful when the children become more animated' (Nafferton), and another (Oundle) presents a 'dull and inert mass' (*PP* 1852: LXXX, 682, 683). Anxieties about the 'unknown public' and incoherence are here focused on the 'inert' pupils who do not demonstrate abilities, or even responsiveness. In such instances the required ethical function of schools, to induce a certain 'animation', is patently allied with the quest for efficiency in the nation. For to make pupils 'animated' and responsive means that they develop new capacities in their lessons and classroom interaction, that inform their later lives; literature's role partly lies in thus 'animating and moving' pupils (S: 89) so that they want to learn. Although some pupils' unruliness requires restraint, regulation of the 'inert' pupils appears even more necessary to make them productive.

The disinterest of the schools' inspectors and teachers was meant to draw out abilities from pupils by developing their motivation and conduct as they became impressed by the adults' example. The interrelationship of ethics and efficiency in this undertaking clearly anticipates the larger complementary roles of culture and the state in Arnold's 1860s' social and political criticism. In his inspector's role, his 'humanizing' work extends to the transformation of uncoordinated and undeveloped capacities in schools across the country. This managerial activity centres on encouraging the use of common resources: at one point he writes how 'it matters little, comparatively, what the text-book is, so long as it be uniformly adopted' (S 27). Similar observations foreground how more integration, both within the self and across the schools, serves a larger project of nation-building. Arnold's index of achievement on both local and national fronts, efficiency, is however not simply based on a goal of economic wealth as it was for many Liberal politicians who were devoted to cost-cutting in government (significantly, the Newcastle Commission's brief in 1858 was to inquire into ' "cheap elementary instruction" ').[5] For Arnold, efficiency is philosophically laden – in the sense of *that which produces effects*, and *causes to be*. In individuals, efficiency signals that identity is *realized* in activity. The notion of activity, and dynamic relationship, are central to his philosophy, and the scandalous subtext of the 'inert' and muddled states is that those (persons, resources, institutions) who are subject to these states are nothing, since they do not realize their own powers.[6]

Arnold's managerial work in education spanned the examination of pupils and pupil-teachers, assessment of morale and resources, acting as an adviser and support to the teachers, writing reports, and interaction with other Inspectors. His co-ordination of these different tasks depended on the quality of practical wisdom or *phronesis*, the term in Aristotle's *Ethics* that denotes the characteristic of those who deal successfully with 'the management of households and nations'.[7] Schools can be seen as an intermediate form of these communities, and Arnold's own efficiency in balancing the different demands, and the different considerations within particular tasks, bears out the importance of classical distance and practical wisdom in his self-invention. A key pointer to this classical derivation is his delineation of a critical sensibility in his writing on the translation of the classical texts that were attributed to Homer, which will be discussed at more length shortly. Here the basis of the 'critical faculty' lies in an ability to see the object as it is, or the 'thing itself', which explicitly requires

> the finest tact, the nicest moderation, the most free, flexible, and elastic spirit imaginable; he should be, indeed, the 'ondayant et divers,' the *undulating and diverse* being of Montaigne. The less he can deal with his object freely and simply, the more things that he has to take into account in dealing with it, – the more, in short, he has to encumber himself, – so much the greater force of spirit he needs to retain his elasticity ... one often sees erudition out of all proportion to its owner's critical faculty.[8]                                   (I: 174)

What is striking about this passage is the emphasis on certain personal characteristics and the hazards of 'erudition' and encumbrance, that suggests how the use of the 'critical faculty' is not simply intended for the critics of poetry that Arnold mentions here. These lines seem more generally a counsel for dealing with the competing claims and informational overload of modern life, and they markedly correspond with Arnold's own *'undulating and diverse'* existence. His school work, including his individual reports, demonstrates his ability in balancing different considerations – how he was not ground down by the 'grinding' work.

His reports envisage literature's role in the development of a 'critical faculty' which similarly converts disorder and incapacity into order and control. In his assessment of pupil-teachers in 1852 literature can thus overcome

> the utter disproportion between the great amount of positive information and the low degree of mental culture and intelligence which they [the pupils] exhibit ... [they] often cannot paraphrase a

plain passage of prose without totally misapprehending it, or write half a page of composition on any subject without falling into gross blunders of taste and expression...the study of portions of the best English authors, and composition, might with advantage be made a part of their regular course of instruction to a much greater degree...Such a training would tend to elevate and humanize a number of young men.... (S: 19–20)

As Arnold here ends his first report in a way that sounds contemptuous – with the 'low degree of mental culture', and 'gross blunders' – he is open to charges of denying social differences, and imposing alien standards. Yet his thinking is directed to helping pupil-teachers to a less restricted life, and a pragmatic, tolerant approach appears in his reports also (in the early 1860s he objects to pupils being penalized for speaking in dialect, for instance). In the context of the proliferation of factual reading matter, he assumes the empowering effects of literary authors' broad views on pupils. Character, and 'cultivation', denote the important ability to stand at a distance from 'positive information' or facts – much like poets should see widely, and critics should deal 'freely and simply'. For Arnold, English literature – even just 'portions of the best English authors' – encourages the needed distance and independence, for elementary pupils, that the privileged classes gain from the classics. The end of confusion and of naïve identification are both seen to depend on these 'portions' which bring pupils in contact with other modes of thinking and feeling than they have encountered so far. This entails a comparative release from ingrained attitudes, so that choice becomes possible. Nevertheless, what Arnold seeks with one hand – pupils' greater independence, their subjective empowerment – he tends to take away with the other, in that his assurance of 'the best authors' and 'gross blunders' suggests that there are objective standards that pupils will come to accept.

In its emphasis on the role of teachers and inspectors, the educational system that he sought resembled the moral supervision that Dr Arnold had exercised at Rugby. Yet his own pursuit of the public good entailed insistence on the interests of the 'mass' of pupils over some exceptional ones. This recalls his 1852 letter that resisted the privilege of the 'gifted'. Under a 'really national system of education', Inspectors would no longer occupy themselves in inquiring with what success the three or four head boys (sons, probably, of tradesmen in good circumstances) out of a school of 100 or 150 children, could work an equation, or refer words to their Greek or Latin constituents. (*S:* 39)

The persistent levelling tendency in Arnold's work appears clearly here as he follows through his disinterested role in this proposal at the outset of his schools' career. His egalitarian liberalism appears not just in his attitudes to pupils but also in his challenge of his fellow-inspectors' practice. While he is intolerant of 'inert' states, and certain forms of popular literature, he is nonetheless resistant to a prevailing form of competitive individualism that seeks the 'success' of the few at the expense of the many.

The inspectors' acceptance of established norms of 'success' – a form of naïve identification with their bureaucratic office, and with their own class position – is seen by Arnold to impede the development of a modern, 'really national system'. The force of his words 'really national system' lies in the desired suspension of established class and occupational standards, to secure a modern state where 'the people' are more integrated. In this context, an assessment of Arnold's later commitment to culture, by the English critics Chris Ryle and Kate Soper, is worth quoting since it also applies to his pedagogy and his inspectorial role: 'self-realisation conceived in terms of the transcendence of naïve identification can also be said to be democratically oriented in its encouragement of reflexivity'.[9] Ryle and Soper insist on the middle-class caste of Arnold's thinking, and it is not necessary to look far to see how ways in which he warrants this profile – as in his prejudices about the 'best English authors'. We have just seen one of the problems with assimilating his educational thinking to middle-class agendas, however – his egalitarian resistance to the competitive individualism in middle-class thinking and practice. His personal 'reflexivity' – or departure from established assumptions – is also evident in his own new recourse to the politically-charged, bureaucratic language of efficiency as a civil servant. In pursuit of efficiency, his early report outdoes many of the other Inspectors in its fervent insistence on a 'really national system of education'.

His routine schools' employment and 'reflexivity' belong in the histories of the growth of the civil service and professionalism in the Victorian period. The status and authority of professional men then became increasingly tied to their disinterested ethos and other intangible assets like educational qualifications. In the next chapter, it will become more apparent how a disinterested stance prevailed in Liberal politics also. The emancipatory effect of a disinterested, professional existence for some individuals should not be underestimated. When Arnold had entered employment as a schools' inspector after having been Lansdowne's private secretary, he experienced personally some of the freedom from patronage that was a mark of the new professionalism. The longstanding rationale for the recruitment of the school inspectors from graduates from Oxford and Cambridge – their capacity for disinterested, objective realism, through their classical education – in fact appears in his 1853 'Preface' when it observes that those who have to do with 'the ancients...are more truly than others under the empire of facts' (P: 668). Even as Arnold displayed this prejudice, such selection was under scrutiny. The *Times'* revelations of government incompetence in the Crimean War in 1854 strengthened the calls for competitive civil service recruitment that were made in 1853 in the Northcote-Trevelyan Report. As things stood then, classical studies in effect bought the graduates into employment as Inspectors. Their intangible assets of education and professionalism were increasingly a source of power.

## MODERN ELEMENTS IN CRITICISM

Arnold's first public appearance as a critic was in November 1857 in the inaugural lecture of his Oxford Poetry Professorship, 'On the Modern Element in Literature'. The ambition and innovation in his performance on the stage of the Sheldonian Theatre make it seem something of a manifesto as well as a début. As he stood back from his school work, he broached the phenomenon of modernity in a lecture that moves over more than two thousand years and several literary genres in considering the value of literature, especially classical literature, in modern society. As if his thinking was nonetheless informed by his educational experience, modernity is here conceptualized both negatively and positively, as a dismal spectacle of

45

confusion and as the emergence of a new society when rational standards and ideas are fruitfully brought to bear on this disorder. Publicity is central to this process which depends not simply on the right ideas but also on an 'intellectual deliverer' who 'communicates' the ideas effectively, so that knowledge issues in action. As he made free with his brief as a poetry professor again in subsequent lectures, Arnold's professorial appointment became a platform for his modern agenda. His first term in the Chair, which lasted for five years, was renewed for a further five years in 1862.

His self-invention now incorporated the idea of himself as an 'intellectual deliverer' – a modern critic who publicizes ideas for the rescue of modernity. The idea of modern confusion that ran across his early poetry and his educational writing remained the fundamental problem that his criticism addressed. We will see how he built up his modern critical role in the five years up to 1862 by proposing ideas that amount to literary, academic and political standards – qualities for the selection of literature; appropriate political practice; and guidelines in translation and the composition of poetry. As part of such engagement, he paid increasing attention to the public and communication, and in one way and another his different texts seek answers to Walter Bagehot's question, how should we speak to 'the many'? His inaugural lecture was poorly received at the time, on the grounds of its unfortunate, dogmatic manner. Arnold echoed this criticism when he eventually saw to its publication in 1869: the style 'is that of the doctor rather than the explorer' (I: 18). On the ground of its dogmatism, the editor of the *Spectator*, Richard Holt Hutton, objected that, for Arnold, 'the thoroughly clear apprehension of a moderately rich experience contributes much more to what is properly the 'modern' element in literature, than the half-clear apprehension of a very much richer experience'.[10]

Not of all of Arnold's early lectures have survived. Some of these lectures were revised and appeared as essays in relatively new journals from 1863, before being collected in his *Essays in Criticism* (First Series), in 1865. This pattern, whereby his texts were first delivered orally, then published as essays in journals that reached a wider public, before book publication finally, characterized much of his production up until *Culture and Anarchy* (1867–8: 1869). His sensitivity to the requirements of his role and to his readership appears over the first publication of his early lectures, in *On Translating Homer* (1861). Here he reluctantly declined the offer of journal publication in *Fraser's Magazine*: 'as they are my first published Oxford lectures it is more decorous to publish them as a book than as magazine articles' (2: 43). The controversy that developed over his views in this work, and his recourse to pamphlet publication in 1859 in 'England and the Italian Question', were both harbingers of his higher publicist profile subsequently.

The prioritization of communication in Arnold's inaugural lecture demonstrates the importance of the public in his understanding of modernity – how transformation entails new relationships between people, with less exclusive practices. His lecture at once identifies him as a modern professor who attends to the public by speaking in English. Though the lectures were open to members of the public, the lectures of previous Poetry Professors had been given in Latin. Privately, Arnold wrote of 'the preposterousness of an Englishman lecturing to Englishmen in a dead language' (1: 36), and he gained permission to abandon the Latin convention from the university authorities. Within the lecture, which discusses several classical authors including Sophocles and Virgil, this gesture towards the modern public is reinforced by allusions to contemporary publicity. These journalistic allusions – the mention of a speech by Prince Albert that was reported in the *Times*, and many references to 'facts' and 'spectacle' – seek to attract interest from his audience and to bring classical learning into direct relation with the life of Victorian society. The lecture's 'plain' language, which involves much repetition and idiomatic expression, underlines this need to accommodate modern audiences. Hence he buttonholes his audience as to the relative merits of the Elizabethan writer, Sir Walter Raleigh, and the ancient Greek historian, Thucydides: 'Which is the ancient here, and which is the modern? . . . Which has the rational appreciation and control of his facts? Which wanders among them helplessly and without a clue? Is it our own countryman, or is it the Greek?' (I: 27). As he avoids literary expression with these direct questions, we have to hear his words, not just their content, to grasp how Arnold's assertion of his own modernity is not separate from his post-poetic stance.

Although his delivery is designed to please an audience from outside the University, his words challenge the ordinary sense that the writer from Elizabethan times, Raleigh, is more modern than Thucydides. Even though he accepts the obsolescence of lecturing in a 'dead' language and uses a plain and idiomatic modern vocabulary ('without a clue'), he nonetheless argues for the continuing value of classical literature, provided it has a 'modern element'. This 'element' is not chronological but normative – not a question of its historical date, but of qualities that have important application in the world around him. As he defines it, this 'element' from the past entails 'the rational appreciation and control' of facts (I: 17), which requires an ability 'to see life whole', and awareness of the 'general ideas' which are the 'law' of these facts (I: 20). This 'element' also signals the communication of these laws, where a plain style and due emotion to reassure and animate readers are important. Literature's function is hence to provide an overview whereby confusion can be structured and made good as latent strengths are realized: to ensure that knowledge is not inert, literature must also motivate readers. This closely echoes Arnold's school reports where certain 'portions' of English literature lead to motivation and self-mastery. More specifically, he now derides the 'mere literary man' who does not connect to, and hence affect, matter: like the 'inert' school pupil, this 'mere literary' individual forestalls efficiency since he avoids creative interaction. As Arnold pronounces which authors are of value across classical and English history on this basis, the 'Modern Element' has something of a manic element in its search for a 'usable' past that repays attention. After this inaugural performance, tutors advised students to avoid his lectures.

The inaugural lecture's importance lies in the way that it establishes the basis of his criticism, where the value of ideas, language and literature is determined by their perceived bearing on society. Its insistence on seeing life 'whole' underlines how objectivity is actually a perspectival feat: 'everywhere there is connexion...no single event, no single literature, is adequately comprehended except in relation to other events, to other literatures' (I: 20-1). In other words, the meaning of texts and historical incidents cannot be understood without seeing how they are related to other texts and events. The discussion of Thucydides illustrates this conditional objectivity as the ancient historian is seen to ply through myth 'to assign their true character to facts, complaining of men's habit of *uncritical* reception of current stories' (I: 26). Here critical realism, whereby dominant frameworks of perception are challenged, appears a condition of objective realism, or objectivity, which reveals the 'true character' of facts. In making the case against '*uncritical* reception', Arnold thus maintains that Thucydides turned away from idealized accounts of the Trojan War to materialist accounts – not honourable oath-keeping about Helen of Troy but shrewd calculation set the Greeks off on their wars. Thucydides' readiness to question 'current stories' leads him to discover empirical evidence (which Arnold does not specify) which overturns the prevailing 'stories'. 'The Modern Element' seems less imaginatively engaged by theory, however – here, the relative importance of idealism and materialism – than by the historian's critical reason as he dares to question beliefs that have the status of myths.

This does not mean that the lecture has no time for general ideas. On the contrary, an 'intellectual deliverance' signals ideas that entail a worldly order of creativity in which confusion is succeeded by order. Arnold's idea of the 'modern' is the outstanding case in point here, as a general idea that refers to both desirable and undesirable forms of modernity. If the word 'modern' is resolutely applied, it functions positively, like a diagnosis, by bringing the relief that naming an uncertain condition brings, and hence effectiveness: to discern a confused 'modern' condition seems half-way to amending it. The constructive, formative power of ideas, like the idea of 'the modern', harks back to Arnold's statement that 'poets must begin with an Idea of the world in order not to be prevailed over by the world's multitudinousness' (1: 128). He was soon exploring the formative capacity of ideas further, and investment in certain shaping ideas – above all, 'culture' – was at the core of his publicist enterprise.

His writing gained momentum as he pursued the idea of himself as a modern critic – an identity that was enhanced by his use of modern transport. In his early years as a school inspector he travelled across the country mostly by train, staying in lodgings overnight, often with his wife and their fast-growing number of children. Until 1858 his only fixed residence was with his wife's parents, in London; to gain extra income he assisted his father-in-law in his work as a judge on circuit in the provinces. On some holidays, and on special assignments, he went to the Continent. Despite this demanding travel and employment, he kept up with new literature and through lobbying his brother-in-law he secured his election to the Athenæum Club in London. From 1856 this Athenæum membership gave him the quiet that he needed to write, and access to books. It also gave him a base from which to cultivate the support that he needed for election to the Oxford Professorship. Quite likely his own sense of 'seeing life whole' grew as he moved about the country and mixed socially in London, Oxford, and other regional centres, besides spending time in ordinary places like provincial station platforms. His extensive travel, wide social encounters and networking activities make him more identifiably a 'modern man' than many Victorian intellectuals.

His work-related travel broadened in six months reporting on schools in France (March–August 1859) for the Newcastle Commission. His first independent publication of his criticism appeared during this assignment – his little-known political pamphlet of August 1859 on 'England and the Italian Question'. His educational work brought him introductions in Parisian literary, intellectual and political society. The politicians that he met who had particular educational importance included François Guizot, the one-time Prime Minister who had in 1833 introduced 'la loi Guizot', a foundational measure in modern French elementary education. In the face of the relatively advanced state of the French educational system, and the several aristocrats who were his superiors in the Education Department back at home, Arnold followed through his roles as a schools' inspector and a modern critic by producing his first political criticism. In England political writing that opposed the aristocracy then still appeared in pamphlet form.'England and the Italian Question' criticizes the English aristocracy for not taking seriously the modern ideas of liberty and equality that had prevailed in the French Revolution of 1789. This pamphlet is an account of England's and France's responses to the Austrian invasion of Italy and the Italian movement for independence, the Risorgimento.

Most importantly here, the pamphlet examines the role of ideas, public opinion and moral sensibility in modern political life. In particular, it sees the foundational importance of 'the people' – or 'the masses', and 'the French nation'– in contemporary politics. And it is preoccupied by questions of publicity – *how* do you speak to 'the many', *who* are they, and *how* are they important? It sees how certain ideas – 'the ideas of religious, political and social freedom' (I: 81) from the French Revolution, the republican calls of Liberty, Equality and Fraternity – have become identified with the ordinary French people. Quite explicitly, the people and the ideas provide the framework of modern politics: 'no politician has played a great part without taking them [the ideas of 1789] into account' (I: 81). The pamphlet outlines how these ideas function as a form of attenuated moral argument which has great ethical force. Yet the prudential note in 'taking them into account' indicates Arnold's sense of these ideas' rhetorical importance as slogans that provide shared reference points and he seems aware of how their repetition may render them meaningless. The claims of the ideas on absolute moral grounds do not prevent politicians from manipulating the people, indeed 'the masses of the people are strongly *susceptible* to certain powerful ideas' (I: 81, my emphasis). The moral force of the ideas may hence be hijacked by politicians who appeal to people's vanity, for instance, in seeing themselves as defenders of freedom. The force of the ideas as slogans – where ideas like freedom appear in headlines – lies in the way that different motives and interests can be grouped under 'one' righteous cause.

Aptly, then, the pamphlet refers repeatedly to 'signs', false-seeming and 'symbols'. The neologism, 'Palmerstonianism', was coined to convey the manipulative use of publicity for political ends by the English Prime Minister at this time, Lord Palmerston. As Arnold observes the political power that the French Emperor derives from a disinterested moral stance, he points up Palmerston's adroitness as a modern politician who is conscious of his newspaper reputation. Karl Marx observed how this aristocratic liberal leader was adept at press manipulation: a posture of disinterest was central to his strategy that apparently substituted ' "phrases for facts, phantasies for realities, and high-sounding pretexts for shabby motives" '.[11] In its enthusiasm for power, Arnold's pamphlet seems, however, unresolved about denigrating the French ruler's instrumentalism and applauding his effectiveness, and hence Palmerston's; with some insouciance, it wonders whether Palmerston's popular championship of Italy was a case of 'felicity' or 'strategy' (I: 93). Louis Napoleon needs to perform 'truth and sincerity' to gain support: popular performance is now a standard requirement of political life. The political ruler who wants to gain the people's support has to encode his own honesty and sincerity to ensure that they are received in this way by others. As it expands on this idea, the pamphlet seems a direct response to Bagehot's exhortation about speaking to 'the many' when it asserts that Louis Napoleon 'not only knows how to speak to the people a language which they will comprehend, but how to speak it with the force and effectiveness of conviction' (I: 81).

The pamphlet demonstrates a preoccupation with questions of style, power and communication that bear on Arnold's own publicity. His instrumental concerns, however, have in general been overshadowed by his famous ideas. In 'The Modern Element', the desire for words to correspond to reality was tempered by awareness of their power to shape reality: the point of an 'intellectual deliverance' is that minds grasp and shape facts through ideas. The 1859 pamphlet shows greater appreciation of the instability of words and their symbolic role in political life. The particular appeal of politics appears here as an arena for creativity, through *praxis*, where the force of ideas – words like liberty and equality – may create new realities in the body politic.

Following the relatively obscure pamphlet, in the lectures that were collected in *On Translating Homer* (January 1861), the performance and controversy that mark Arnold's work as a publicist began to be pronounced. Especially since he was contemplating a second five years in the Professorship, perhaps, the first lecture was projected in order to overcome 'complaints that I did not enough lecture on poetry' (I: 239). But while he tried to allay objections to his subject matter, critics found his approach exceptionable. Opinion about the series of three lectures that ensued was divided between censure of its dogmatism, rudeness and egotism, and enthusiasm for the open discussion of Homer and its rejection of scholarship that seemed pedantic. For Hutton, Arnold was here especially the 'cut-and-dried man of culture'. Arnold's fiercest and most longstanding critic, Fitzjames Stephen at the *Saturday Review*, protested against 'the tone of the lectures', their breach of decorum: 'some things in them...are not the sort of things which an Oxford Professor ought to deliver officially before the University'.[12]

The subject of Homeric translation was then dominated by the work of the German scholar, Friedrich Wolf, which maintained that the Homeric texts had been produced through oral retelling, rather than by any one author. Such recitation, and their verse-form in hexameters, indicated that the classical texts bore the imprint of ordinary people from ancient times rather than privileged individuals. Particular controversy hence centred on the value and identity of these texts in translation. The claims of generalists and specialists were at issue, and the politics of texts: how should the historical and popular aspects of these texts be rendered now? In view of the way that Arnold's thinking and writing were shortly dedicated to a different 'translation' of ideas and knowledge to the 'general public', this discussion prefigures his emergence in a stronger publicist role.

His lectures were written in reaction to the scholarly translation of the ancient Greek texts that had been brought out by John Henry Newman's brother, Francis Newman. For Francis Newman, his scholarly translation (which needed a glossary for readers) had democratic credentials since it rejected established norms of fluency, that were tied to established interests. In that the lack of fluency in his strange translation broke with the experience of privileged readers, it seemed faithful to a new audience of the people. For Arnold, on the contrary, the obscurity of Francis Newman's work meant that it was barely accessible to most people.

Arnold's argument is directed against pedantry as it upholds the importance of the effect of a Homeric text as a whole; yet it keeps the 'general public' at a distance, as the proper translator aims 'to reproduce on the intelligent scholar, as nearly as he can, the general effect of Homer' (I: 118). Again in his argument Arnold here maintains the value of seeing the object as it is, in its entirety. In Homer's case this entails fidelity to the values of his 1853 'Preface': 'plain and direct' thought and expression (I: 102), and also 'nobleness', that appears in 'the grand style' (I: 103, 116). In addition, a proper translation of Homer, which depends on 'duly penetrating' oneself in Homer's qualities, requires rapidity (I: 102–3). The activity of sympathetic penetration requires distance from the translator's own ingrained feelings, or subjectivity; and later on, in the passage that was quoted from earlier in this chapter, Arnold elaborates the ideal exercise of tact and flexibility in response to 'poetic truth...of all things the most volatile, elusive, and evanescent' (I: 174). To illustrate his point, he observes how a nineteenth-century writer such as John Ruskin attributes a 'kind of sentimentality, eminently modern', to Homer: unless a modern translator 'feels him [Homer] truly, how can he render him truly?' (I: 103; 1: 101). While Arnold emphatically disclaims the possibility of accurate knowledge of the past at the start of his *Homer*, this rejection of 'modern' sentimentality demonstrates his historical sense and hence something of the inconsistency that runs through this work especially. If we cannot know the past, how can we know that Ruskin is so misguided?

The importance of this work in Arnold's evolution can be seen in the way that his later three-fold division of modern audiences into scholars, intelligent readers and the general public is dimly outlined here. As he comes towards the end of his first five years as professor, his concerns about translation – especially the relationship between scholars and the public – suggest that he is turning over possibilities in his own future. Here he dismisses the idea that 'the proper aim' of a translator' should be 'to stimulate in any manner possible the general public' (I: 118). His consciousness of boundaries and his public image extends to his worldly awareness that it is 'more decorous to publish' his lectures on Homer in a book than in magazine articles. Yet this restraint on Arnold's part was at some odds with his lectures' resistance to the type of 'the pedantic scholar' in universities (I: 118), and their stimulating effect, which derived not only from their range and boldness but also their rudeness towards Francis Newman. For the critic, George Saintsbury, at the end of the nineteenth century, nothing like this series' 'positive critical quality' and 'germinal influence' had been seen for a long time in English literary criticism; its 'synoptic' method, 'sudden-zig-zags' and 'provocation' especially made for wide influence and stimulus.[13] *Homer*'s recognition of literature as a 'living intellectual influence' further foreshadows Arnold's turn to wider audiences in journalism very shortly (I: 140).

Fitzjames Stephen pointed to his deficient reasoning – the way that Arnold did not explain terms that he used frequently, like 'noble' and 'the grand style' (*CHPW*: 93). Arnold's reasoning was tautologous, especially where he used short extracts from writers that he admired – what he later called 'touchstones' – simply to demonstrate the qualities and value that he sought. His idea of 'touchstones' was developed in his essay on 'The Study of Poetry ' in 1880, and it became central to twentieth-century English teaching in schools, where diverse key passages that were meant to reveal certain qualities and values were assembled in anthologies. The idea that particular 'touchstones' operate in this way illustrates quite clearly Arnold's habitual tendency to claim objective authority for his subjective impressions. The particular notion that 'touchstones' are generally agreed 'is simply against common sense that mine will be identical with yours, or with Arnold's'.[14]

Yet despite the conservatism in his impressionistic approach, we will see how he later promoted the re-valuation of accepted literary judgements in his *Essays in Criticism*: if his 'touchstones' seem absolute in the context of classical literature, their precariousness appears in these *Essays*. And although his fairly conformist judgements publicize received opinions about the quality of Homer, just in making explicit the judgements about what was tacit for many ex-public school readers he subjected literature to new scrutiny and possible revision. The unorthodox aspect of his lecturing was heightened by his striking first-person voice. This especially incensed Stephen, who remonstrated against 'the way the "I" always comes in – an authoritative, oracular way, something akin, we venture to guess, to "the grand style" ' (*CHPW*: 96): Arnold had gone on the platform like an old hand, and played to his audience's prejudices.

The 'flair' he displayed here was the exuberant face of his tact in 'Democracy'. His care in the writing of this essay in 1861 is indicative of the subject's importance and his concern to persuade his readers; much of his difficulty in writing it centred on how 'It needs so much tact as to how much and how little to say' (2: 62). The fact that this essay was destined for his first book, his private publication of his Newcastle report, *The Popular Education of France*, also encouraged him to take great care in writing. The essay resembles *Democracy in America*, the mid-century two-volume study by the French political theorist, Alexis de Tocqueville, as well as Arnold's own earlier pamphlet, in that it is premised on the decline of the aristocracy and hence the decline of 'high ideals' (II: 17). Like the pamphlet, it maintains how 'the masses of people in this country are preparing to take a much more active part than formerly in controlling its destinies' (II: 15). In sum, it argues that 'for some time at any rate' (II: 15), social and political weakness can be averted through state provision of schools that will induce proper 'public character' in the new ruling middle classes. Here values and facts can be reconciled as this 'public character' will maintain ideal standards *and* legitimate middle class rule for 'the masses' (II: 11). As the middle classes will be modernized by taking on the breadth that is needed for stable rule, this reformation is the precondition for the extension of 'public education'. In thus attempting to tie middle-class political rule to education through the cultivation, or culture, of the middle classes, this essay anticipates the ambition of *Culture and Anarchy*, which urges an expanded version of culture on the aristocracy and the working classes also.

'Democracy' illustrates the politicization that civil servants were prone to undergo in their executive work. Arnold's criticism tries to bear on contemporary English politics in its ambition for more state intervention *and*, quite practically, in its wooing of the middle classes to achieve this goal. Its extended beginning attempts to persuade readers by acknowledging their fears as it labours how 'No sensible man will lightly go counter to an opinion firmly held by a great body of his countrymen' (II: 3). The essay lacks explicit political references to particular politicians but its goal of more state intervention was a party political matter that divided Liberal politicians.

Arnold's immediate task in 1861 is to get the middle classes to endorse public education, and hence to attach them to the idea of the state: 'the nation may...acquire in the State an ideal of high reason and right feeling, representing its best self...and forming a rallying-point for the intelligence and for the worthiest instincts of the community, which will herein find a true bond of union' (II: 19). In contrast, American education is held up in the full text of *The Popular Education* for the absence of 'a salutary standard' – any 'beacon to the imagination of thousands' (II: 161). While the English middle classes need to be attached to the idea of the state at this juncture, 'Democracy' makes a point of validating the desire for equality in *all* those who seek it by explicitly refuting the view that this desire is unworthy of some individuals. Further, 'the incapacity of aristocracies for ideas' – a key tenet of Arnold's subsequent class analysis – is here specifically seen to retard the crowd's transformation into a people. Since they will give no ground to the modern spirit and the ideas of 1789, 'they [the aristocrats] leave the people still the multitude, the crowd' (I: 11). Ideas in these different forms are accordingly pivotal for social transformation in this foundational essay of Arnold's social and political criticism. Far from being simply related to reason, they are invested with emotion and force for social reformation, as 'rallying-points' or slogans; a kind of poetry.

'Democracy' thus advances a political project through a pragmatic reading of present circumstances. As it delineates the legitimate, egalitarian consciousness of 'the masses' at length, the essay appeals directly to middle-class readers: 'Can it be denied, that to be heavily over-shadowed, to be profoundly insignificant, has, on the whole, a depressing and benumbing effect on the character?' (II: 9). A whole page of such eloquent psychological appeals potentially dispels class altogether, however, by hailing middle-class readers in a more or less buried life of oppression that they also know. Its fierce antipathy to subordination, and specifically its notion of the English 'democracy' 'throwing off the tutelage of aristocracy', links this writing to the essay, 'What is Enlightenment?' by the Enlightenment philosopher, Immanuel Kant. The universalist tenor in 'Democracy' manifests a pull to a different, more equal order, rather than simply a more contained one, for it adumbrates a place *without* class distinctions. When it presents 'persons without extraordinary gifts or exceptional energy, and who will ever require, in order to make the best of themselves, encouragement and directly favouring circumstances' (II: 9), it touches on experiences of under-privilege and lack of recognition that cross class boundaries. The sensitivity to the way lives can be 'stunted', and the affirmation of an 'effort *to affirm one's own essence* ... to be neither cramped nor overshadowed' (II: 7), suggest how Arnold's eloquence has to do with his own suffering as a child, as we glimpsed earlier.

Through this essay it is apparent how he continues to think in terms of a re-constructed *public* sphere, rather than a particular class project as such. Its immediate objective is the management of social change through middle-class education, and it acknowledges the pertinence of class differences. Its language points beyond such differences to an equal society, however, as it creates a moral atmosphere with compelling force. While the essay allows for equal protection under the law, and differing social classes at present, democracy itself appears as a rather abstract state that is to be realized through successive waves of the best self until a whole society of public-minded citizens puts paid to law altogether by embodying it in themselves.

In the vagueness, inconsistency and idealism of this account, Arnold's weaknesses as a political thinker are apparent. His failure to ground a common culture on much more than a particular ethical schooling and moral sense seems one of the largest obstacles to taking him seriously as a political thinker today. Yet the sense of a common humanity that underpins his later writing about culture is not only important in itself, it is an undeniable force in modern politics. In such 'moral discourse, thinness and intensity go together', according to a recent analyst of moral argument, and his ability to create this kind of moral atmosphere is central to Arnold's identity as a modern publicist.[15] *Culture and Anarchy* is in many respects a comprehensive gloss on this earlier essay (which Arnold republished in 1879), and its resemblance is not simply intellectual. Significantly, in view of its emotive power, 'Democracy' was taken up in American magazines in the 1890s, where it became a key text in the battle for educational reform to achieve greater equality.[16] Very few copies of *The Popular Education* were sold in England, however, and Arnold had to reimburse the publisher. His serious practical intent appears in his request that the Liberal Chancellor, W. E. Gladstone, should take note of the essay, to swerve from the broad policy of *laissez-faire* in education.

In the ten years since he had become a schools' inspector,

Arnold had established his main ideas as a modern critic, which hinged on his conception of ideas' formative power and their necessary application to modern society. His work in education taught him the role of agreed ideas and standards in shaping modern life quite practically. His early proposition, that 'Poets must begin with an Idea of the world in order not to be prevailed over by the world's multitudinousness', was transposed to modern society in his inaugural lecture, and then it was fleshed out in relation to different areas of modern life, including politics. More than with *'making'* poetic objects, he became preoccupied with making new social and political arrangements, that constituted a different form of creativity. In accord with his belief in *praxis* and objective realism, his criticism demonstrated a two-way traffic, as he not only articulated certain ideas but also gathered ideas – including those about authority and effectiveness – from history, literature and the contemporary world. He thus moved between real and ideal worlds – between how things are and how they may be regulated. In his fast-emerging identity as a publicist he would increasingly put his accounts to use in promoting his ideas with the general public.

# 3

# The Theatre of Operations: Publicity, Criticism, Culture, 1862–1869

*For the Englishman in general is like my friend the Member of Parliament, and believes, point-blank, that for a thing to be an anomaly is no objection to it* (III: 268)

...for a people like ours, with a strong fund of imagination genius and humour, are best reached by sometimes being audacious and giving oneself free play. But what I more and more try to get, is the desire for the triumph of ideas...(2: 360)

Following his turn to journalism in 1862, Arnold produced two books, *Essays in Criticism* and *Culture and Anarchy*, which were to influence debates about literature and culture well into the twentieth century. In these books he strengthened his interpretation of modernity by turning his attention to modern literature and by developing his social and political views. The traces of this work can today be seen in the circulation of some of their well-known catchwords – 'disinterestedness', 'the free play of the mind', 'Philistines', 'sweetness and light', 'the best ideas' and 'culture'. The first appearance of these books as separate essays in journals – often after they had been delivered as lectures – was typical of Arnold's publication from 1862. The different *Essays in Criticism* first came out in five different English journals (1863–64; 1865), and the six chapters of *Culture and Anarchy* initially appeared in instalments in the *Cornhill Magazine* (1867–68; 1869). The 1860s saw the growth of new journals that reached a large middle-class audience and Arnold's new role as a periodical journalist tells of his concern to achieve widespread influence. Other periodical essays that he had written were collected in *A French Eton* (1863–64; 1864) and in his book, *On the Study of Celtic Literature* (1866; 1867).

Both the *Essays in Criticism* and *Culture and Anarchy* maintain the importance of communication, and in *Culture and Anarchy* 'the great men of culture' are described as publicists – 'those who have had a passion for diffusing, for making prevail, for carrying from one end of society to the other, the best knowledge, the best ideas of their time ' (V: 113). This much-quoted passage elaborates how these 'great men of culture' have laboured to make knowledge 'efficient outside the clique of the cultivated and learned' (V: 113) and here the word 'efficient' obviously connects this undertaking to Arnold's continuing educational work. A similar role of *making* ideas and knowledge more widely available is assigned to critics in the *Essays in Criticism*. This emphasis on the business of publicity in these books, and their own continuing publicity – their enduring currency as critical literature – at once make them central texts when considering Arnold's evolution as a publicist, and their further claims to attention will become evident. Arnold's promotion of his ideas in this writing was in fact a focus of literary criticism in the 1930s and 1940s which took up the view of the poet and critic, T.S. Eliot, that Arnold is 'a propagandist for criticism'.[1]

When he became committed to publicity through journalism in the 1860s Arnold inaugurated the custom by which professors of literature at Oxford speak to wide audiences – John Bailey, Terry Eagleton and John Carey are recent examples; yet his writing is distinctive in its many allusions to politicians. Despite such political references and his concern with social wellbeing, influential critics see Arnold as disengaged from politics. Two recent critics of Arnold's work, Robert Young and Francis Mulhern, have both seen his central idea of culture as opposed to political life. For Young, Arnoldian culture is 'a mental place outside society', for instance, while Francis Mulhern situates this culture in a tradition of aesthetic knowledge of a 'richly differentiated whole' that neglects 'the art of the possible'.[2] This chapter suggests how such negative views depend on a restricted definition of politics and a restricted understanding of *Culture and Anarchy* as an intervention in Victorian political debate. It suggests how readings of Arnold as divorced from

61

politics neglect his continuing educational aims and his negotiation of his different roles. It outlines how his different roles need to be taken into account when considering his criticism, and how he resembled contemporary politicians in his use of publicity for political purposes. His most explicit party political essay, 'The Twice Revised Code' of March 1862, will be given particular attention since it established enduring features of his political criticism as well as the terms – or rather, the lasting constraint – on which, as a civil servant, he subsequently wrote social and political criticism. Here especially it is apparent how his educational work sustained his cultural polemic.

Publicity was important not only in Arnold's understanding of modern transformation and for diffusing his ideas, but also for his reflexive practice. While he sought publicity for the sake of influence, he depended on the publicity that his writing received as he developed his thinking polemically through engaging with his critics. His methods also changed in response to his writing's reception. His essay on 'My Countrymen', in February 1866, used the device of European viewpoints in response to criticism of his essay on 'The Function of Criticism at the Present Time' (November 1864). Reading his criticism chronologically helps to convey his reactive writing practice. With the *Essays in Criticism*, this chronological approach will extend to reading 'The Function of Criticism' after the writing that it 'introduces'. Arnold's prolific and various production in the 1860s prevents sustained attention to the timing and interweaving of his different journal publications as such, however, and his work will mostly be discussed in the order of its book publication. But at the outset it is appropriate to relax this broadly chronological approach in order to establish his journalistic profile, and the political and journalistic contexts of his writing.

## ARNOLD, JOURNALISM AND POLITICS

In many ways Arnold's critical career was synchronized with developments in journalism and politics from the mid-nineteenth century and he was empowered by taking up opportunities that journalism presented. In the 1850s he had abandoned his early habit of viewing newspapers as a worldly distraction. In the 1860s, his growing political interests can be seen in the frequency of references to journalism in his correspondence and criticism. Like politicians, he saw the importance of journalism in influencing public opinion and, therefore, the ways that people might vote. His political pamphlet on the 'Italian Question' and his privately-printed report, *The Popular Education of France*, had each had very limited sales. In his first, anonymous, journal publication, 'The Twice Revised Code' (March, 1862), Arnold turned to the long-established *Fraser's Magazine* to sway opinion against an educational measure that had been proposed by the reactionary, anti-democratic Liberal politician, Robert Lowe.

Arnold's correspondence demonstrates his great investment in journalism as a vehicle for the diffusion of ideas so that they become widely accessible. In this basic, informative function, journalism helped to create an integrated nation by establishing common knowledge. He foregrounded this function to his mother in describing how his 'Twice Revised Code' presents 'the subject [the Code] in its *essence*, free from those details with which it is generally encumbered and which make "outsiders" so afraid of it' (2: 123). His imagined audience moves from 'outsiders' to insiders, however, when he speculates whether his 'Twice Revised Code' has influenced certain politicians, such as the politician Lord Derby, a conservative leader who had earlier been Prime Minister (2: 125). As we will see, Arnold's 1860s criticism is often uncertainly pitched between a usual audience of the general public and more specialist readers, especially party politicians.

His essays also shift between relatively steady, informative writing to more purposive prose that is less straightforward. When he had seen popular forms of writing as an 'engine' in 1848 he had enthused how, 'amongst a *people* of readers the literatture is a greater engine than the philosophy' (1: 92). Typically, such 'engine' work proceeds for him either through creating an uplifting atmosphere in writing, or else more personally, through using shame or gentler methods. He frequently envisages his writing in the 1860s as '*getting at* the English public – such a public as it is, and such a work as one wants to do with it' (2: 238). This role as an outspoken, gadfly-type journalist alternated with a gentler, tactful approach. Despite his enthusiasm at the prospect of what journalism might do, however, he persistently had doubts about the capacity of the public ('such a public') to be moved in the way that he wanted.

In his periodical journalism after 'The Twice Revised Code', he clearly wanted to be identified by his publications. As the most obvious step to this, unusually among periodical writers then, he cultivated personal influence by seeking publication in journals where he was permitted to sign his work. His inaugural lecture had conceded the great appeal of 'persons and character' in narrative (1: 35). By the time of *On Translating Homer* Arnold had himself become known as a personality. His journalism continues this pattern as a means of gaining attention and influence. There had been discussion about ending the policy of anonymous journalism since the 1830s yet journalistic anonymity continued well into the 1870s. Even so, from the outset Arnold prioritized journals where his authorship was visible from his signature, and he explained to the French literary critic, Sainte-Beuve, that he had chosen *Fraser's Magazine* for the publication of his lecture on 'A Modern French Poet' (January 1863) as it was 'almost the only literary journal in England where the writer could sign his article' (III: 407). When *Culture and Anarchy* appeared in the *Cornhill*, Arnold was virtually the sole named contributor.

His practical sense can be gathered from the speed with which his prose was taken up in the changing journalistic marketplace. In the case of his book publication, Bill Bell has established how his correspondence with the publisher, Alexander Macmillan, demonstrates some desire to avoid self-publicity. But in his essays in journals, Arnold's exhibition of personality unabashedly contributed to the emergence of 'personal journalism' and his own fame. When the Cambridge philosopher, Henry Sidgwick, identified him as 'a favourite comedian', in his 1867 review of the first part of *Culture and Anarchy*, he pointed to Arnold's reliance on personality, which Sidgwick related specifically to the abandonment of journalistic anonymity (*CHPW*: 110). The term 'personal journalism' was used in the 1880s with reference to writers as well as writing – the greater individuality of writers, as well as the new 'human interest' that journalism provided, that conflicted with the impersonal norms of serious public discourse.[3] Especially through signing his name, and his distinctive informal style that included sarcastic allusions to public figures, Arnold contributed to this new journalistic phenomenon. From 1863 his essays generally went into the newer magazines – entertaining journals such as *Macmillan's Magazine* and the *Cornhill Magazine*, where essays on politics were mixed with fiction.

Arnold's informal, personal methods in writing were dependent on the growing informality in journalism generally that extended to political representation. In the late 1840s, political writing in the main metropolitan daily newspapers, like the *Daily News* and *The Times*, had mainly consisted of lengthy reporting of Parliamentary debates and editorial comment. While politics might be discussed quite abstractly in the leading quarterly reviews, there was little topical discussion of politics apart from newspaper editorials.[4] From 1855 the new weekly and monthly reviews and magazines began to include topical political commentary. As these journals increased the visibility of politics, they began to supplement daily newspapers in the work of influencing public opinion. The foundation of the literary clubland paper, the *Pall Mall Gazette*, in 1865, brought more reflective, topical political comment into the daily press also. The growth of such political writing was a sign of the lightening of journalism generally. This in turn reflected its changing commercial basis as sharper competition and greater need for capital investment – especially for the latest technology in printing – made high sales more imperative. *Macmillan's* and the *Cornhill* were both founded in the winter of 1859-60 and the latter soon achieved sales of 120,000. Even though these figures could not be sustained, the circulation of more substantial periodicals such as the *Contemporary Review* was relatively small in comparison.

A succession of leading Liberal politicians – Palmerston, Lord John Russell and William Ewart Gladstone – were quick to try to turn the developments in the daily press to their advantage, and as journalism became more reliant on advertising and capital investment, particular associations between newspapers and politicians developed.[5] The cultural analyst, John Thompson, describes the broad change in terms of a new 'mediated political field' where politicians became visible to the public. Palmerston's aptitude in presenting a disinterested public image that worked to his advantage was glimpsed in the previous chapter. In the 1850s and 1860s, the media presence of politicians depended on their ethical stance more than obvious signs of personality. In the development of mass meetings that were addressed by politicians and then reported in the press, the centrality of journalism to modern democracy was especially evident. The new possibilities of a public profile were displayed in Gladstone's career above all. In 1861 he became 'The People's William' in the Liberal *Daily Telegraph* for abolishing the tax on paper. This newspaper exploited the symbolic value of this act that marked the end of the socially repressive 'taxes on knowledge'. The abolition had actually come about from Gladstone's fiscal policy of cutting taxes in his role as Chancellor of the Exchequer.

The paper's spin in this case illustrates how the 'mediated political field' operated to the advantage of politicians who could establish their moral credentials with the public, and how particular phrases became slogans in newspapers in this process. Educational policy became caught up in such political publicity when the slogan 'payment by results' was applied to Lowe's 'Revised Code'. Arnold's publicity became tied to phrases that resemble such journalistic slogans and catchwords – what the twentieth-century French cultural analyst, Pierre Bourdieu, has described in an academic context as 'intellectual rumour – labels of schools, truncated quotations, functioning as slogans in celebration or polemics'.[6]

As politicians cultivated resources that gave them authority with a wider public, a disinterested stance became more important in the Liberal party. Journalism's heightened commercial basis coincided with this moralization of liberal politics. It was from this moralization, and politics' new visibility and informality in journalism, that a form of cultural politics emerged. Here electoral politics became newly determined by considerations of moral sensibility in public opinion. Recent historical studies foreground how liberal politics proceeded on the basis of a disinterested stance in the 1850s and 1860s. The subordination of sectional interests for the national good, and a principled approach to politics, were key components of this national strand of Liberalism. The historian Patrick Joyce contentiously elaborates a variant of such non-sectarian Liberal feeling, in which, further, a sense of equality informed a 'democratic imaginary' from the mid-century in the politics that were associated with the ex-Chartist popular Liberal, John Bright, and Gladstone. The key point about this 'imaginary' is that interlinked 'figures/forms/images' bring a 'feeling of living in a democratic culture and society', and this 'imaginary' configuration is operative in actual political life.[7] *Culture and Anarchy* will be seen as both manifesting and appealing to non-sectarian feeling, against an individualistic version of liberalism that centred on free trade.

Discussion of Arnold's writings will demonstrate his closeness to Liberal publicity in their call for disinterest, their personalized approach to politics and their use of catch-phrases and emotive writing in journals. His collected *Letters* demonstrate his keen political interests. He mixed with influential politicians socially, including the conservative leader, Benjamin Disraeli, and Gladstone. He was on especially friendly terms with the Liberal MP Grant Duff, and he regularly conversed with leading men in education and the law. Many references to W.E. Forster in his collected *Letters* indicate how closely he followed the public appearances of this politician, a Liberal MP who became Education Minister from 1868, who was married to his older sister, Jane. In his early writing Arnold had sometimes speculated about taking up politics. His letters suggest his sense of marginality beside politicians, which was exacerbated by Forster's importance, and also by Arnold's awareness that the Irish philosopher Edmund Burke had managed to be both a critic and an MP. Forster appears to Arnold as a parliamentary 'organ of a great transformation' or 'movement' in the 'English spirit' in 1863, and Arnold adds at once, 'I shall do what I can for this movement in literature; freer perhaps in that sphere' (2: 244). Yet Arnold's challenge to the Nonconformists in the middle classes may have contributed to his failure to gain promotion in the Department of Education in 1869. Such ambition and his political allusions indicate that he was not so much above political affairs as more marginal to them than he wished, which made effectiveness in writing more urgent.[8]

## FROM 'THE TWICE REVISED CODE' TO *A FRENCH ETON*

'The Twice Revised Code' anticipates Arnold's subsequent publicist activity in its attack on 'mechanical' state action though it nonetheless upholds increasing state control of education. The reactionary liberal, Robert Lowe, was then the House of Commons' Vice-President of the Committee on Education. He produced the Revised Code in 1861 in official response to the Newcastle Commission's recommendations on elementary education. The new Code proposed to provide better 'popular education' and to reduce the bureaucracy in state funding by tying the grant allocation for elementary schools to the success of school pupils in tests in the three 'R's' – reading, writing and arithmetic. The unstated aims here, of a reduction in government expenditure and the retrenchment of state activity, would in future also be served by teachers' payment from local management committees rather than the Education Department. Instead of being salaried civil servants employed by the central office, the teachers would be paid – and summarily dismissed, in some failing schools – by these local bodies. The teachers' status would be reduced further by reductions in their training, in concession to the view that the education of the people was pitched at too high a level.

The Revised Code was based on belief in free trade among Liberal politicians. This approach, which dismissed a broad liberal education for the people for the sake of cheap labour, underlay Lowe's boast, 'If it is not cheap, it shall be efficient; if it is not efficient, it shall be cheap'.[9] The Code aroused intense press reaction. Arnold's essay in *Fraser's Magazine* vehemently attacked the proposals for change. It especially objected to weaker support for schools as institutions, the reliance on the examination of pupils for school funding, and the inadequacy of such examination in three subjects. Like his subsequent school reports, it complained bitterly about the effects of 'payment by results' upon pupils and teachers, and also upon inspection.

Against a 'mechanical' approach, 'The Twice Revised Code' upholds elementary schooling as an ethical, civilizing process: a school is 'a living whole with complex functions, religious, moral and intellectual' (II: 224). Even in assessment, differences in the condition of pupils and schools make '*well* and *ill*...

relative terms' (II: 236). The new Code is not only inept, but unethical, since the shift of principle in the move to base funding on examinations (a 'Prize-scheme') foregoes the idea of state responsibility in favour of a system that is, in effect, based on prizes ('a gratuitous boon of *prizes*', II: 240–1). While increased accountability is necessary, the school fabric should be supported regardless of 'results'. Arnold entirely accepts the need for reform, yet he suggests the existing system should continue until 'the mind of the country' is 'ripe' for more considered change (II: 240). His case against the Code ranges from the narrowing effects of the mechanization of teaching to its financial implication of a two-fifth reduction in the education budget. His matter-of-fact rhetoric, with a point-by-point approach, extends to the consideration of motives and intentions: '2. Why its authors are trying to do this' (II: 213). In his essay's many-sided attack, the ability to see things as a whole, in general, appears as a political virtue.

Here, exceptionally, Arnold's apparently disinterested thought as an expert issued in partisan political publicity, in opposition to his superior, Lowe. While his views reflected his position as a schools' inspector, his writing in *Fraser's* however violated the unstated convention that civil servants should not intervene in a matter of government policy by writing for the public. The anonymity of his essay evidently did not mask his authorship for those who knew his work. In these circumstances, his habitual concern with the question, *how do you write for the public?*, not surprisingly comes to the fore in his essay, for his role as a critic and as a neutral civil servant were in tension. It was not simply a case of his speaking up courageously for what he believed, at some risk to his employment, since his public utterance was in some conflict with his own belief in the public sphere. The anomaly in his intervention was highlighted by a book of 1864 by the disaffected Liberal politician, Earl Grey. This insisted that civil servants should not take part in public controversy, or write for the newspapers, as had happened recently. It seems likely that Grey was referring to Arnold, who had not only opposed the Revised Code in *Fraser's* but also in a letter in the *Daily News* that was signed from 'A LOVER OF LIGHT'.

The consequences of his disregard of civil service protocols were unclear to Arnold and he wondered if his superiors would 'make my place uncomfortable' (II: 350–1). He presented his essay as a simplified version of the eighty-page pamphlet that Sir James Kay-Shuttleworth had produced. Kay-Shuttleworth had presided over the educational Inspectors for ten years before Arnold joined the service. Although he had retired from this post in 1849, his writing on public education still carried authority. Arnold's fidelity to the civil service is juxtaposed with his role as a citizen in spreading the knowledge on which opinion is based as he maintains how his mastery of the facts enables the general public 'to form an opinion' upon the Code: in contrast, Kay-Shuttleworth's report enables 'everyone who has to *discuss* the new Code . . . to go deeply into the subject' (II: 212-13). By representing his essay as an abstract of information for the general public, from Kay-Shuttleworth's long pamphlet for MPs, Arnold attempted to mitigate the unorthodoxy of his own activity.

Yet it seems that he also produced his anti-Code publicity for the MPs who had not actually read Kay-Shuttleworth's eighty pages. Cross-floor voting was then common in Parliament, and Disraeli apparently sought 'just such a brief to speak from' (2: 125). Moreover, Kay-Shuttleworth sent a pamphlet copy of the 'Twice Revised Code' to every MP. Arnold's personal attacks – on Lowe ('growing desperate'), the Dissenters (who are seen to lack intelligence) and other groups ('the selfish vulgar of the upper classes', for instance) – advanced the personalization of Victorian politics in journalism and a culture of name-calling and slogans (II: 243). His letter in the *Daily News* on the day of the full Parliamentary debate was a further flagrant intervention in the Parliamentary process. In the event, Arnold and other anti-Code writers only succeeded in modifying the Code, so that a third of the public funding for schools became based on school attendance.

Nonetheless, his use of his 'vivacities' to publicize the narrow, materialistic outlook of some politicians and sections of the middle classes became a central feature of his later 1860s social and political writing. His acute animus against the narrow-mindedness of the middle classes, and specifically against free-trade liberalism, also dates from this political episode, and this intensified in subsequent years as he experienced the effects of the Code in his daily school work.

Central features of his later social and political criticism appear in outline here, such as his attention to the role of the press, his insistence on less precipitate political action, and his affirmation of the state's responsibility towards the disadvantaged.

More immediately, the unacceptability of his criticism of Liberal policy on the Code contributed to his use of less explicit methods of political criticism. At intervals throughout the 1860s his correspondence alludes apprehensively to the adverse reaction to his 'Twice Revised Code – for instance, how this made his appointment on the Taunton Commission less likely. His opposition to the Code in his general schools report in January 1862 had itself led to the censorship of that report. The continuing civil service and Government sensitivity to criticism of Government policy in fact led to suspicions of more widespread censorship of reports and charges against Lowe 'of improperly altering or mutilating the Inspectors' Reports' (Super, 2: 310–11). Arnold continued to seek more state educational provision, and to complain about the Revised Code in his school reports. However his subsequent journalism for the general public avoided detailed discussion of the many specific political proposals in education in these years and his insistence on the separation of disinterested ideas and political practice cannot be dissociated from his office as a civil servant.

His many allusions to current events and public figures in his 'Twice Revised Code' echoed the practice of writers in the 'Condition of England' debate, such as Thomas Carlyle, the English social critic who had once visited Dr Arnold at Rugby. The debate in Victorian periodicals and fiction was about the significance and alleviation of poverty, and the wide gap between the rich and the poor. Arnold here joined this debate politically by publicly exposing Lowe's economic priorities, the materialist outlook of the middle-classes, and the shortcomings of all who neglect the public interest and the condition of disadvantaged children in schools. His confession to Jane in 1858, that the public provides 'the stimulus necessary to enable me to produce my best – all that I have in me, whatever that may be' (1: 402) had apparently referred to his poetry. Yet the range and extroverted performance of his political writing later in the 1860s suggest the psychological warrant that speaking 'disinterestedly to 'the public' in criticism gave him (II: 243). Literary disinterestedness was more customarily manifest in 'liberal heroics', or self-dramatization, that took the form of self-abnegation, yet for Arnold 'disinterested' criticism for the public licenses his 'all' – his own variousness, that is, including his aggression.[10]

In Arnold's next journal essays on education, which resulted in *A French Eton* (June 1864, after serial publication in journals), he significantly abandoned outspokeness for indirect methods of influence on middle-class education. Privately he emphasized his tact and attempt to *'persuade'* – 'how necessary it was to keep down many and many sharp and telling things that rise to one's lips' (II: 370). In his praise of a transformed middle class he eschewed 'sharp and telling things' for flattery: 'what a power there will be, what an element of new life for England!' (II: 322). On the horizon after this, there is the fate of the 'lower class' in a strange peroration about 'This obscure embryo, only just beginning to move, travailing in labour and darkness... Children of the future, whose day has not yet dawned' (II: 324).

In his role of mid-wife to a reformed society that can be glimpsed here, Arnold capitalized on the topical interest in the aristocratic school, Eton, to publicize his case for state provision of secondary education along the lines of a model French lycée – hence the title. As in 'Democracy', his case turned on the need for the middle-class to develop a more disinterested ethos through education, as a precondition of comprehensive social and political transformation. By amplifying the inadequacies of middle-class education at present – partly through comparison with French schooling – this book indirectly contributed to the appointment of a Government inquiry into middle-class education, the Taunton Commission, on which Arnold hoped to serve. Its special targets included the numerous middle-class 'Educational Homes' for '20 *l.* a year'. To highlight the absurdity of these establishments, their advertisements in the *Times* are quoted out of context, where they take on the aspect of Dickensian satire – 'Education, 20*l.* per annum, no extras. Diet unlimited, and of the best description' (III: 281). Such schools

> can't give that which they 'conscientiously offer' – And why? Because they want the securities which, to make them produce even half of what they offer, are indispensable – the securities of supervision and publicity. (II: 282)

This passage refers to the lack of public knowledge of middle-class schools, and Arnold elaborates the role of 'learned corporations' and public examinations in providing such publicity. The governmental function of publicity is explicit in this educational context. Perhaps because he increasingly indicted the modern press, Arnold's political thinking is not readily associated with the positive role of publicity and public opinion in modern politics and administration.

His own criticism nonetheless came to rely on publicity to expose apparent inadequacies, and so to mobilize opinion. He ensured that copies of *A French Eton* went to influential politicians, including Gladstone. The book's impact was such that Lowe and another leading Liberal politician in education, Lord Granville, publicly dissented from its case for state control of secondary education. Such public debate contributed to Arnold's growing controversial reputation (see Super, II: 372).

## ESSAYS IN CRITICISM

The essays in Arnold's next book, *Essays in Criticism* (c. February 1865) were first published in journals between January 1863 and November 1864, during which time *A French Eton* appeared in instalments. His new literary essays similarly rely on an undogmatic, flexible manner to advance his ideas – now, about the importance of modern European literature rather than classical literature in modern society. The *Essays in Criticism* mainly discusses writing and writers since the medieval period, and its subjects include the French writers, Maurice and Eugénie de Guérin and Joseph Joubert, the Dutch philosopher, Baruch Spinoza, and the German poet and critic, Heinrich Heine. The subsequent uptake of this book had to do with its informal style and biographical approach, and, especially, its presentation of literary, social and political ideas that had considerable plausibility. The idea that 'the English poetry of the first quarter of this [nineteenth] century [Romantic poetry] ... did not know enough' (III: 262), for instance, is only one of many opinions that Arnold put forward that still reverberate in English criticism.

The unusual focus on European writers by an English critic in the 1860s reflected his wide reading, and his understanding of the 'public sphere' and modernity, whose horizons were both for him international – or rather, European – as well as his belief in literature's social importance. For the French Revolution of 1789 is here clearly the foundational event of modernity, and the course of English and European history is seen to depend on publicity of one sort or another. The judgment that the English Romantic poets did not know enough is accordingly tied to the idea that the French Revolution took place hastily, without a sustaining 'culture and force of learning'. Though the topsoil seemed ready, the ground was unready for the ideas of 1789 to root in practice; as they were without proper intellectual nourishment themselves, the Romantic poets could not nourish others. In the light of the history and prospect of social and political transformation, 'The Function of Criticism' accordingly requires critics to ascertain and spread 'the best ideas', to create a 'culture and force of learning and criticism'; and the best creative writers must combine these ideas, 'presenting them in the most effective and attractive combinations', whereby they create a 'glow of thought and life' (III: 260, 263). Elsewhere in the *Essays*, a literary work can act as a 'critical hit' (III: 278), and the best 'hits' have 'critical power', whereby they are 'capable of emitting a life-giving stimulus' (III: 183). If this language suggests advertising jargon, Arnold's instrumental approach to writing makes this apt. *On Translating Homer* had observed how English literature ranked after the literatures of France and Germany as a 'living intellectual influence' (I: 140) and the idea of writing as an 'engine' of transformation informs these *Essays*.

A more personal reason for his focus on the European writers, was that – apparently in remedy of *On Translating Homer*'s dogmatism – Arnold was better able to write in a fresh, unforced way on these subjects than on authors whose importance was already established and/or controversial in England. 'The Function of Criticism' indeed confesses how criticism may sometimes 'have to deal with a subject-matter so familiar that fresh knowledge is out of the question' (III: 281). In the competitive marketplace of the new monthly journals, where novelty was sought increasingly, his 'fresh' writing was in demand from editors and it capitalized on the new availability of European texts. The importance of particular writers in the *Essays* is accordingly at issue. Literature emerges as a site of struggle, where Arnold seeks to challenge prevailing judgements. His revisionist ambition appears in an early essay: 'To all who love poetry, [Maurice de] Guérin deserves to be something more than a name' (III: 15).

The *Essays'* more particular interest here lies in Arnold's articulation of his ideas about modern literature at greater length than previously. Though many of his ideas were far from new, they were developed and tested through the essays' serial publication. His most striking lesson from his testing method was the advisability of excluding his controversial early essay, 'The Bishop and the Philosopher' (January 1863), from the 1865 collection. This essay, on a book by the Bishop, Bishop Colenso, analyzes the conditions of modern literary production, including the role of journals in spreading ideas in English culture. Readers are divided into professional scholars, informed readers and the general public. This account allows for both a 'special professional criticism' – the assessments of theologians, philosophers and historians – and 'a general literary criticism' (III: 41). *Essays in Criticism* displays similar variety as they move across history, religion, philosophy, poetry and prose, and it is with reference to all 'literary works' in the humanities that the 'Arnoldian' function of criticism emerges clearly in 'The Bishop': 'Literary criticism's most important function is to try books as to the influence which they are calculated to have upon the general culture of single nations or the world at large' (III: 41). The essay suggests that Colenso's book is unsuitable for the general public, or 'the many', since they are not emotionally prepared to deal with his advanced reasoning. Colenso is attacked relentlessly, and the general public's special need for emotional edification is underlined by quotations from authorities that include the Bible, Plato and Spinoza. As a result, Arnold was first here heavily criticized for elitism – for writing that was 'abominably bumptious, swaggering, & illiberal'.[11] 'The Bishop' in fact maintains the need to recognize differences in readerships for effective communication, but its blunt presentation of the difference between 'the few' and 'the many' backfired on this count as it alienated general readers. It seems Arnold's desire to avoid controversy at this stage played a smaller part in the essay's lack of re-publication than his awareness that his target was 'too easy' (Super, III: 417). His thinking from this essay appeared in a revised form in 'The Function of Criticism'.

The withholding of 'The Bishop' in response to criticism points to the other respect in which the *Essays in Criticism* is important here, Arnold's pursuit of publicity and influence through his study of other writing. The word 'power' recurs in his prose as he moves between reflection and practice in search of writing that has effects on others. Brief consideration of his writing on Maurice de Guérin, Heinrich Heine and Joseph Joubert demonstrates his conflicted belief in literature's modern social and political importance, his attention to versions of prose that he seems to learn from, and his preoccupation with the identity of modern readers.

'Maurice de Guérin', on a French nineteenth-century nature writer, shows Arnold continuing to worry about the social significance of art that had preoccupied him as a young poet. This essay reiterates the idea in his 1853 'Preface' that a pure literary art is maladjusted to contemporary life. As if Arnold cannot allay his anxieties about his own writing for the modern public, variations of this theme occur in most of the essays. As a poet, Arnold rejoices in Guérin's ability in 'catching and rendering every rustle of Nature' (III: 30) – a 'magical power' (III: 14), from an aesthetic mode of knowing that is inclusive and sensual:

> The grand power of poetry is its interpretative power; by which I mean, not a power of drawing out in black and white an explanation of the mystery of the universe, but the power of so dealing with things as to awaken in us a wonderfully full, new, and intimate sense of them, and of our relations with them. (III: 12–13)

Reading 'poetry' is here above all a moving experience in which objects are seen afresh, in an unfamiliar way. Yet during the essay Guérin's genius is devalued. His intensity becomes a sign of a pathological, 'devouring temperament' (III: 32): 'he lived like a man possessed' (III: 34). Through such banal pathologization, which plays on Guérin's reputed death from consumption, or tuberculosis, Arnold pursues his thesis that poetic intensity must be postponed since we live in an 'unpoetical' age, where there are more urgent calls than pure literary art. Guérin 'hovers over the tumult of life, but does not really put his hand to it' (III: 31).

'Heinrich Heine' demonstrates further how literature is valued by Arnold for its social effectiveness in translating modern ideas into practice. He is presented as a writer who effectively advances a sceptical disposition – 'the modern spirit'. In this respect he is seen to resemble another German author, Goethe, who

> is absolutely fatal to all routine thinking; he puts the standard, once for all, inside every man instead of outside him; when he is told, such a thing must be so... he answers with Olympian politeness, "But *is* it so? Is it so to *me?*" Nothing could be more really subversive of the foundations on which the old European order rested; and it may be remarked that no persons are so radically detached from this order, no persons so thoroughly modern, as those who have felt Goethe's influence most deeply. (III: 110)

Despite this resemblance, Goethe's radical detachment and ultimate value are distinguished from Heine's worldly position. As a worker in literature's modern 'theatre of operations' (III: 122), Heine puts an end to ideas being treated as merely 'counters or marbles, to be played with for their own sake' (III: 120). To convey such mental foreclosure readily, Arnold introduces the word 'Philistine'. He used the label repeatedly in his subsequent criticism, to publicize and undermine what he saw as the closed minds of the middle class, and especially the English Nonconformists – Christians who were outside the established Church of England. Through his humorous literary prose, Heine is seen to induce German people to open their minds and adopt a sceptical, critical attitude. A modern publicist, he moves society towards greater equality through devices like humour and irony that get under his readers' defences. As we learn how he turned away from 'direct political action' against 'the German Governments', and his 'propagandism took another, a more truly literary character' (III: 119), he seems a model for Arnold's professional role as a civil servant who cannot be *seen* to undertake partisan political work; Heine represents, rather, the force of indirect 'political action' in writing.

The reclusive French writer, Joseph Joubert, apparently endorses Arnold's own use of plain, vernacular words:

It is by means of familiar words that style takes hold of the reader and gets possession of him. It is by means of these that great thoughts get currency and pass for true metal, like gold and silver which have had a recognised stamp put upon them. They beget confidence in the man who, in order to make his thoughts more clearly perceived, uses them....' (III: 195)

Arnold's translation of Joubert's words suggests how writers should present their ideas for common circulation so as to acquire credibility. His words imply a two-way process, however, as a writer's style evidently 'gets possession' of readers partly on account of the way that 'familiar words' 'get possession' of him – much as Arnold has himself been 'got' by the familiarity of recognized passages in his touchstone-like extracts. 'Joubert' proceeds to draw out the distinction that is implicit here, which preoccupies Arnold, between writing that resembles Coleridge's and writing that is more like Joubert's, which is pitched towards readers. Coleridge's ultimate importance is contrasted with Joubert's 'more appreciable, immediate effect...upon formed personages to whom the present belongs, and who are actually moving society' (III: 193). While Joubert's has less 'power and richness' than the other kind, it has more 'tact and penetration' – terms that Arnold frequently employs in writing about his own criticism. As he elaborates further how Joubert's approach 'was more *possible* than Coleridge's, and more receivable' (III: 193), he seems another writer whom Arnold learns from for his own art of the 'possible' in 'moving society'.

His heightening sense of writing that appeals to the powerful, seen here, suggests how 'formed personages' have limited receptivity to ideas and hence require specific personal methods to disarm them. The sudden appearance of 'formed personages' as a category in 'Joubert' nicely indicates the variability and tentativeness of Arnold's taxonomy, and how his *Essays* not only reiterate and rationalize his former thinking but also how they apparently stumble on new ideas. His core categories of social belonging, and readers, change between different texts, so that the categories of social class alternate with more old-fashioned terms like 'the multitude', 'the few and the many' and 'the common people'.

As Arnold persistently imagines modern readers, nonetheless, his earlier understanding of the force of ideas for modern peoples is developed. While it seems that the 'formed personages' need telling attacks that 'get at' them, *or* tact, for ideas to get through to them, the 'many' remain open to the moral force and implications of ideas. Indeed the exposition of philosophical ideas will not even be listened to by 'mankind at large', 'unless it first learns what their author was driving at with them, and finds that this object of his is one with which it sympathises, one, at any rate, which commands attention' (III: 175). Arnold's essay on 'Spinoza and the Bible', here, in effect elaborates his own approach in 'The Twice Revised Code'. That essay had tried to expose the cost-cutting and discreditable change of principle that was 'driving' Lowe's proposal. His withheld essay on 'The Bishop and the Philosopher' presents moral force explicitly as an agent of transformation, in a passage where such force seems ripe for transfer to a political context: it was not by 'intellectual truth' that 'the Reformation touched and advanced the multitude: it was by the moral truth of its protest against the sale of indulgences, and the scandalous lives of many of the clergy' (III: 44). In this and other instances, one function of his literary criticism for Arnold seems to be to amplify his existing beliefs about the role of moral force.

In the *Essays* artistic, intellectual and political, instrumental concerns are thus mixed in the course of Arnold's attention to the power of literary works in modernity. This preoccupation with effectiveness has largely been eclipsed by the particular ideas that the *Essays* puts forward. However his belief in the power of different forms of writing contributes to his challenge to a traditional account of creativity in the *Essays'* introduction:

> men may have the sense of exercising...free creative activity in other ways than producing great works of literature or art; if it were not so, all but a very few men would be shut out from the true happiness of all men. They may have it in well-doing, they may have it in learning, they may have it even in criticising (III: 260).

The essay from which this passage comes, 'The Function of Criticism at the Present Time', is the essay that Arnold's 1853 'Preface' failed to be, inasmuch as it relates how critical writing is currently more needed than creative writing. The assertion of critics' 'sense' of creativity is one aspect of this re-evaluation of traditional belief.

The importance of 'The Function of Criticism' in the teaching of English came to rest on such elevation of criticism which requires the 'free play of the mind' and 'disinterestedness', and these qualities are at the centre of the present renewal of interest in Arnold in America.[12] Generally speaking, to be disinterested is *not* to be without interest but to approach an issue without prejudice, in detachment from one's *particular* interests. The operation of the liberal public sphere formally rests on such elevation in informed discussion. 'The Function of Criticism' specifically upholds such disinterestedness against the allegiance of 'Philistine' Liberal MPs to the Liberal party line ('"let us all stick to each other, and back each other up"', III: 276). More memorably, intellectual disinterestedness is celebrated in Edmund Burke. So we see how, at the end of his laborious historical study on the French Revolution, he is 'irresistibly carried...by the current of thought to the opposite side of the question' (III: 267), so that he changes his views about the Revolution. This image became an icon of liberal open-mindedness in twentieth-century criticism.

But though 'The Function of Criticism' upholds rational processes of persuasion, argument and influence which require the spread of ideas through books and journalism in the public sphere, it also displays a contrasting type of publicity in its outburst against two Liberal politicians. In this passage Arnold can be seen more strenuously *making* public the shortcomings of Liberal politics by speaking as a publicist *for* a wider public, as its representative. To take up the terms of a recent historical account of the press, his allegiance here shifts from an informative, steady mode of polite public address – a kind of reasonableness which Burke epitomizes – to a representative mode, in which he tries to speak disinterestedly on behalf of the underprivileged.[13]

To understand his outburst, we can unpack the differing forms of disinterestedness in this essay. The introduction outlines a flexible, literary mode, in which explicit judgement is suspended:

> it is by communicating fresh knowledge, and letting his own judgment pass along with it, – but insensibly, and in the second place, not the first, as a sort of companion and clue, not as an abstract lawgiver, – that the critic will generally do most good to his

readers ... the great safeguard is never to let oneself become abstract
(III: 283)

'Insensibly' allows for effects that operate beneath observation, as sounds and images exert force and 'touch' others. This kind of disinterestedness, that is embedded in the senses, is pitched against the 'abstract law-giver' who alienates audiences. Its enunciation here is in a line from *On Translating Homer*'s advocacy of the 'finest tact, the nicest moderation' – '*undulating and diverse* being' (I: 174). The particular association of Arnold with urbanity arises from his demonstration of such qualities.

Such writing differs from disinterested *criticism*, which requires abstraction from 'practical considerations'. Suspension of partisanship, and not speaking on behalf of a constituency, are crucial here:

> The rule may be summed up in one word – *disinterestedness*. And how is criticism to show disinterestedness? By keeping aloof from what is called 'the practical view of things'; by resolutely following the law of its own nature, which is to be a free play of the mind on all subjects which it touches. By steadily refusing to lend itself to any of those ulterior, political, practical considerations about ideas, which plenty of people will attach to them ...                    (III: 270)

The question about how to 'show' disinterestedness is here itself an issue of modern publicity – of how something appears in public so as to be effective. Not only civil servants who worked for the state, and members of the professions, but the editors of journals and even the Liberal Party all claimed forms of disinterest. Arnold specifically seeks 'language innocent enough' to spread the view that the English constitution is 'a colossal machine for the manufacture of Philistines' (III: 275). This question about how to 'show' disinterest arises in the contexts that have been sketched, where the proliferation of disinterested stances in practice meant that these stances could lose authority *as* disinterest. A historical moment that was marked by all sorts of practical interests in disinterestedness informs his question as he contemplates the institution of Parliament. Arnold's statement about disinterestedness tacitly invokes the neutrality of the civil servant for the critic. In context, it is essentially a call for the importance of ideas, and hence the need for action to be driven by policy, rather than

Philistine economics that are *only* practical. But the formulation about 'show' is contaminated by Arnold's awareness that disinterestedness is itself a source of authority and so not divorced from practice.

In these circumstances, 'The Function of Criticism' not surprisingly conflates different forms of disinterestedness. In addition to the kinds of disinterestedness that are identified in the extracts above, there is a further literary kind of disinterestedness that entails the 'free play' of the senses. While the free play of the mind that Arnold upholds in Burke deals in arguments and ideas, Arnold's own exhibition of aesthetic free play follows the sounds and associations of a single word, the name of a woman. The counterpart to the exemplary, disembodied Burke of the public sphere is this woman from the workhouse, 'Wragg': where Burke is pure mind – an eminent public intellectual – Wragg is all body, a liminal figure.[14] Like a Condition-of-England writer, Arnold brings her into the essay for objective realism – as a fact that needs to be considered for a whole, or accurate, political picture. He mentions Wragg in the first place to refute two Liberal politicians' myths of progress – to expose their hypocrisy and inaccuracy that mask social deprivation. He juxtaposes newspaper reports of the politicians' speeches about the 'best race' and 'ideal perfection' in England with reports of a child 'found dead in the Mapperley Hills', which state that 'Wragg is in custody'. To the politicians' exultant claims he opposes the stark representation of these material facts, with 'the final touch, – short, bleak, and inhuman: *Wragg is in custody.* The sex lost in the confusion...' (III: 274).

Yet from seeking Wragg's inclusion in a liberal account of the condition of England, and more humane conditions, hence more humane representations, Arnold veers into aural play which is apparently prompted by her name, which sounded the same as a menstrual towel, a rag:

> what a touch of grossness in our race...such hideous names, – Higginbottom, Stiggins, Bugg! In Ionia and Attica they were luckier in this respect than 'the best race in the world'; by the Illisus there was no Wragg, poor thing! And 'our unrivalled happiness;' – what an element of grimness, bareness, and hideousness mixes with it and blurs it; the workhouse, the dismal Mapperley Hills. (III: 273)

Though the presence of Wragg in this essay begins in protest against inaccuracy and deprivation, this insistent, sexually-charged word-play entails this woman's further objectification. Such free play conveys Arnold's pleasure in his revulsion. Yet his quotation of Liberal politicians, free association, exclamation marks and repetition put language on parade, so that his words have a parodic effect and we may wonder, quite who is speaking here? In other words, the free association of words highlights the dissociation of 'Wragg' from human and sexual being in the newspaper reports and her non-existence for the politicians. The free play based on seeing her *only* in sexual terms accentuates the actual *denial* of her sexual being, in life and in the press – the brutality that surrounds Wragg. Fitzjames Stephen's literal-minded criticism missed the point by proposing that Arnold was merely seeking a different, more indirect, literary way of 'putting it' ('Wragg is in custody', *CHPW*: 119). Arnold's insistence that 'there is profit for the spirit in such contrasts', and his retention of his offensive utterance in the publication of the *Essays*, suggest that the violence that women like Wragg experience may only be adequately conveyed by a breach of decorum. His writing about Wragg concludes that only by a 'small circle' who convey truths like "Wragg is in custody" under their breath will 'adequate ideas...ever get current at all ' (III: 274).

Arnold produced Wragg in the first place as an emotive symbol of hypocrisy and deprivation – like an investigative journalist who waves the counter-evidence. In the 1880s such sensationalism would become associated with the campaigning journalist W.T. Stead, then the editor of the *Pall Mall Gazette*. Arnold acknowledged in his essay how one of his political targets, the Liberal politician Mr Roebuck, would have 'a poor opinion' of his methods (III: 274) and indeed Wragg brought him notoriety. To view his unorthodox publicist methods as merely complicit with exploitation is to neglect his challenge to established forms of publicity, however. His sensational approach challenges the abstract, generalizing language of the public sphere, and the recurrent rupture of polite discourse is a feature of Arnold's contradictory writing as a publicist and critic. Bourdieu usefully describes the political problem of accredited, 'disinterested' political discourse: 'Political analysis presupposes distance, height, the overview of the observer who places himself above the hurly-burly, or the objectivity of the historian'.[15] Such detachment assumes the cultivation of certain abilities through education or social privilege. Arnold's blunt, moral and personalizing criticism about Wragg abandons distance and seemingly attempts to *show* disinterest by breaking with polite norms as it reads like sensational journalism. He uses exaggeration, a personal case and moral force, as if he is trying to get a political campaign going, to change the sensibility of the public and politicians.

Though 'The Function' tries to distinguish between critical and literary activity, and between ideas and practice, it hence mixes them as it spans different forms of disinterest and publicity. A letter that Arnold wrote in December 1864 confirms his ambitions for literature to change public sensibility: 'I turn more and more towards indirect and gradual modes of action – such as literature. People's spirits must be changed, before their public habits' (II: 361). The anxiety about a pure literary art that we have glimpsed in his *Essays* generally signals a writer who is less remote from current literary concerns than he often appears since he speaks to unresolved claims about the roles of art and politics.[16] As he here prioritizes society and politics, and hence publicity, the repetition of key terms like 'disinterestedness' and 'the free play of mind', and the use of symbols, start to form a distinct Arnoldian rhetoric which paralleled the development of political party slogans.

As if Arnold now embraced the idea of his writing as a 'theatre of operations' for battle against his enemies, the polemical strain that can be seen in 'The Function of Criticism' increased in his subsequent social and political criticism. Immediately before the *Essays in Criticism* was published early in 1865 he produced a polemical 'Preface' for the book in response to criticisms of some of the essays in their journal form. His short virtuoso piece moves between drama, fantasy, satire and panegyric, and here Arnold's rhetorical effect 'becomes so intense, the world so ludicrous, that it's a wonder he stops short of nihilism'.[17] One part of this essay, for instance, attacks the demoralized Philistine middle class by satirically exposing the limits of their materialistic beliefs. A comic scene plays on their anxieties over their own mortality as homeward-bound commuters on a train after a stabbing on 'one of the Great Eastern Lines – the Woodford branch' (III: 288). The drama, visual imagination and bathos of this satiric scene of jumpy commuters anticipate subsequent visual technology and political satire on television a century later.

## FROM 'MY COUNTRYMEN' TO 'THE FERMENTING MIND' OF *CULTURE AND ANARCHY*

The growing engagement with the public and publicity in Arnold's critical career culminated in the experimentation and heightened ambition of his writing from 1866 to 1869, and his most far-reaching book, *Culture and Anarchy*. His sense of self-importance had not lessened in seven months' travel in 1865 on the Taunton Commission to inspect secondary schools and universities across France, Germany, Italy and Switzerland. His Government report, *Schools and Universities on the Continent*, was published as a book by the publishing house of Macmillan in March 1868. His other publications in this period included a series of lectures that were collected in *On the Study of Celtic Literature*; the essays in the *Cornhill Magazine* that were in 1869 made up into *Culture and Anarchy*; and many of the satiric letters on contemporary English politics in the *Pall Mall Gazette*, that were published in *Friendship's Garland* in 1871. In addition he produced general reports as a Schools Inspector, as well as a number of miscellaneous pieces. The heavy burden of his varied kinds of work meant that much of his writing fell behind deadlines.

The movement between, and within, the sometimes over-lapping roles of schools' inspector, government official, Oxford Professor of Poetry (until the summer of 1867), critic and polemical journalist required continual adjustments in the style of his writing and also its content. In this respect he was by now a much-practised publicist who shifted his methods and emphases according to context. His contrasting accounts of the English middle class at this time indicate his flexible, pragmatic approach quite distinctly. In his Taunton report, where national efficiency was a priority, he advanced his case for secondary education in the humanities and sciences by presenting the English middle class as 'cut in two', in professional and business groupings (IV: 309): the former lack scientific or technical knowledge, the latter lack qualities of leadership. The promotion of liberal national unity in *Culture and Anarchy*, however, led to a different representation of a relatively homogenous middle class whose members have strengths and weaknesses in common. We will shortly examine Arnold's self-image as a modern political publicist and the significance of *Culture and Anarchy* as *an Essay in Social and Political Criticism* at a time when publicity was newly important in politics. The immediate personal background of his book lies in his versatility as a publicist – his inter-linked publicity against the English Philistines in 'My Countrymen' and his public writing on education.

His shifting between different professional voices was increasingly replicated in critical writing that used irony, imitation and parody to undermine the views of 'formed personages'. From his essay on 'My Countrymen', these personalizing literary devices made his criticism read more like fiction at the same time that it became newly centred on politics. This resounding essay in the *Cornhill* in February 1866 uses the dramatic device of foreigners' points of view in polemical response to the insularity of Fitzjames Stephen's criticism of 'The Function of Criticism'. As the writing of 'My Countrymen' was delayed by Arnold's Continental travel, it grew into a broad political indictment of English backwardness. This essay's impact led to Arnold writing a series of satiric letters to the *Pall Mall Gazette* that similarly used satire and foreigners' viewpoints to criticize the English, which were published in 1871 in *Friendship's Garland*. The popular author, Mrs Oliphant, conveys the unusualness of Arnold's personal, satiric method here: 'Is it amusement – is it instruction?' (*CHPW*: 254).

The focus of 'My Countrymen' is the confinement and closed-mindedness that Arnold loosely identified with the middle class, the 'Philistines' – the term that now became central to his reputation. As an ironic compendium of European points of view, his highly topical essay criticizes the jingoism, complacency, materialism, ignorance, limited education, religion, journalism and free-trade politics of the politically ascendant middle class. His polemical representation of middle-class weaknesses and vices, where particular politicians and newspapers are named, drew responses from educationalists such as Kay-Shuttleworth as well as John Bright, several other public figures and many newspapers. As was his habit, he described such success to his mother: "'Most of the ... weekly newspapers mention it as the event of the *Cornhill* ... [Thomas] Carlyle also approves, I hear; I am going to see him. The country newspapers have had a great deal about it' (V: 362).

Against the 'clap-trap' of political life – in particular a recent speech by Robert Lowe – and the abject conditions of 'the common people', the essay upholds a moral, utilitarian standard of modernity: 'What is the modern problem: to make human life, the life of society, all through, more natural and rational; to have the greatest possible number of one's nation happy' (V: 18). In a further inflammatory speech about democracy in March 1866, Lowe would call the working classes drunken and venal, unreflecting and violent. From a different standpoint, Arnold's essay participates in this political culture of name-calling. He had initially planned that it would advance state secondary education, but through his European travel it grew into this morally-based political criticism that points towards a welfare state. At present, the conditions of 'the common people' are uncivilized and inhumane; and the middle class is obsessed with 'industry, trade and wealth' (V: 18, 19). Arnold links these philistines to religious Nonconformity in his mention of teetotalism, where his language is similar to that in his school reports after the Revised Code – 'blunted', 'narrow, unintelligent', and without 'stimulus':

> Drugged with business, your middle class seems to have its sense blunted for any stimulus besides, except religion; it has a religion narrow, unintelligent, repulsive ... the very lowest form of intelligential life which one can imagine as saving. What other enjoyments have they? ... in their evenings, for a great treat, a lecture on teetotalism and nunneries. Compare it with the life of our middle class as you have seen it on the Rhine this summer, or at Lausanne, or at Zurich (V: 19)

The unfavourable comparison of England with a European country was one of Arnold's main tactics in helping to create a more Europhile sensibility and to undermine English philistinism. Here he gestures selectively to Swiss and German social life to suit his purpose in highlighting an English work ethic. In its lack of consideration of the official restrictions that Nonconformists had suffered (they were, for instance, still unable to attend the ancient universities), this criticism is typical of his approach to the Nonconformists before 1869.

In addition to its publicisation of philistine shortcomings, 'My Countrymen' is important for its awareness of the centrality of publicity and public opinion in modern politics (V: 18). It registers in particular how the press can be used to simulate public opinion rather than simply to represent it – so that what appears in the press seems to *be* public opinion. The essay was written after Palmerston's death in the Autumn of 1865, and it focuses on the illusory foundation of this liberal Prime Minister's power in his apparent ability to mirror public opinion – to be seen, by the middle class, as ' "our best impersonation" ' (V: 10); 'Lord Palmerston was England' (V: 9). Arnold's earlier analysis of the 'susceptibility' of the people to ideas under Palmerston, in 'England and the Italian Question' (1859), evidently still holds. His satire, now, turns on how claims of Palmerston's greatness are confounded by the actual decline in England's international reputation under his leadership; and the superficial sense in which he represented the public (V: 9–10).

In this political and journalistic context, Arnold's educational writing tries to wrest the opinion of the public, civil servants and MPs from philistinism and a political charade, towards more systematic, rational and ethical educational provision. His educational work not only underpins the political thinking in *Culture and Anarchy* and 'My Countrymen'. It also demonstrates his attempt to advance political objectives in education through public writing. Because of his 'State-views', he had had to overcome considerable opposition to secure his appointment to the Taunton Commission (Super, IV: 345–6), and his long report became a platform for these views. In August 1867 a copy was 'on hand' in the House of Commons, in advance of the publication of the whole Taunton report (Super, IV: 350). Arnold solicited book publication for the wider public by giving a copy of his report to the publisher, Alexander Macmillan, and all the seven hundred and fifty copies of the ensuing book were sold. Its detailed account of practice and policy includes specific recommendations for English education, such as compulsory school attendance (which was introduced in England in 1880).

Arnold used the 'Preface' to *Schools* for an opportunistic, polemical attack on the Revised Code. Criticisms of this Code then dominated his ordinary school reports. These reports emphasize the low morale of teachers, and how the counter-productive regulations of 1862 attempt 'to lay down, to the very letter, the requirements which shall be satisfied in order to earn grants. The teacher, in consequence, is led to think, not about teaching his subject, but about managing to hit those require-ments' (S: 140). Though they technically became available to the public as parliamentary papers, it seems these general reports were only read by other civil servants and interested MPs. In his authoritative book on *Schools*, Arnold is however able to convey criticisms of the Code to the general public, as part of its broad 'Preface', without strictly breaking with the required neutrality of civil servants. Here, as part of its attack on the Code, *Schools* recommends the Continental practice of attending to public support for teachers, despite the attitude that it is 'un-English to regard the mass of the public, the parents of school-children, instead of regarding influential managers' (IV: 24). Arnold's early school reports had wanted parents to be kept at a distance from schools, but now he solicits their support in view of the power of public opinion.

In this context, and in the light of his longer-term thinking about modernity, Arnold self-consciously adopted the role of a new political publicist in the *Cornhill* essays that became *Culture and Anarchy: An Essay in Social and Political Criticism*. In a period in which public opinion was newly important, he perceived the opportunity for criticism that advances a disinterested sensi-bility to exert political force. At a number of points *Culture and Anarchy* suggests the role of publicists in changing sensibility. For instance it distinguishes between those who 'indoctrinate the masses with the set of ideas and judgments constituting the creed of their own profession or party' (V: 112), and culture, which seeks 'to make all men live in an atmosphere of sweetness and light' (V: 113). Arnold's own practice apparently now rested on this distinction between publicity that prescribes 'sets' of ideas and publicity that frees up the 'atmosphere'. Later in his book this distinction is tellingly recast in the opposition between politicians who currently 'educate men's minds...Mr. Disraeli educates, Mr. Bright educates, Mr. Beales educates', and 'the sovereign educators' who open up new ways of thinking (V: 229). The book's lack of enthusiasm for the 'education' and 'creeds' of party politicians is offset by its dedication to the importance of publicity and we will see how *Cultural and Anarchy* undermines free-trade liberalism.

The first chapter of *Culture and Anarchy* was a revision of an essay on 'Culture and Its Enemies' in the *Cornhill* of July 1867, that Arnold had delivered as his last lecture as the Oxford Professor of Poetry. The substantial public reception of this essay underlay his private boast, 'People say to me that I am "a power"' (3: 194). By this time most periodical readers were familiar with his views and there was little notice of the other essays and his book when it came out. The substantial reviews of 'Culture and its Enemies' included one from the Positivist critic, Frederick Harrison, and another from the philosopher, Henry Sidgwick. For Sidgwick, Arnold's identity as a publicist and entertainer was particularly apparent. Sidgwick and Harrison both observed the essay's vagueness, elitism and remoteness from present social needs. Both also identified its self-regarding, egotistical, supercilious aspects: in Harrison's critical 'dialogue', Arnold's culture was marked by 'lurking traces of your superlative dandyism, some of your flabby religious phrases, your hash of metaphysical old bones' (*CHPW*: 226). In his wish to '"gather up all the murmurings into one and see what they come to"' (V: 410), Arnold delayed writing his planned sequel, and his response in the *Cornhill* in the New Year grew in four further essays by September 1868. Such stalled composition means that some readers apparently never get to Arnold's more considered thinking in answer to his critics, since they do not get to the end of *Culture and Anarchy* (whereas 'The Function of Criticism' *introduces* readers to his revised views in the *Essays in Criticism*).

*Culture and Anarchy* seeks to overcome the confusion and waste in modern society through the spread of culture. Its six chapters elaborate this idea of culture, which is much more than the condition of cultivation that appears in Arnold's early school reports (though in all its manifestations Arnoldian culture maintains the importance of striving for human development). Initially, culture is presented as a good that is based on two aspects of the self, 'the sheer desire to see things as they are' and 'impulses towards action, help and beneficence, the desire for removing human error, clearing human confusion, and diminishing human misery' (V: 91). Arnold moves from this two-sided foundation to establish further aspects of culture within the first chapter and then in the subsequent chapters. In phrases whose ordinariness or 'familiar' character seems almost studied at times, culture comes to denote, for example, 'the study of perfection', 'not a having and a resting, but a being and becoming', 'right reason', and 'sweetness and light'. Much of the time culture is defined negatively, by what it is not: for instance, culture does not admit 'the notion of a one thing needful, a one side in us to be made uppermost, the disregard of a full and harmonious development of ourselves' (V: 180).

As culture moves from an ethical condition and pursuit to take on wider national significance, it appears in a racially-inflected dialectic across history. Here legalistic, duty-bound, action-minded 'Hebraic' elements alternate with spontaneous, intellectual 'Hellenic' free play. The loose use of these anthro-pological-seeming terms extends Arnold's 'familiar' approach, as different characteristics are discussed almost as if they come from different family lines. Over the course of the book, culture thus mutates between a category of consciousness, an ethical pursuit of perfection, a historical process, a body of artefacts and a practice of publicity.

The two sides of culture meet in the passage that celebrates the 'great men of culture' who want 'the best knowledge, the best ideas' to 'prevail':

> The great men of culture are those who have had a passion for diffusing, for making prevail, for carrying from one end of society to the other, the best knowledge, the best ideas of their time; who have laboured to divest knowledge of all that was harsh, uncouth, difficult, abstract, professional, exclusive; to humanise it, to make it efficient outside of the clique of the cultivated and learned, yet still remaining the *best* knowledge and thought of the time, and a true source, therefore, of sweetness and light... (V: 113)

Culture's identity includes inner composure and a 'best self' who leaves class affiliations behind – a self that 'rises' above class allegiances. Here the social side of culture appears in diffusion that entails publicity. It is shortly before this passage that Arnold writes as if publicists contend with politicians, by distinguishing between politicians' creeds and parties, and culture, which seeks 'an atmosphere of sweetness and light' (V: 113).

The commitment to 'atmosphere' and the vagueness of *Culture and Anarchy* can make it seem a 'Hellenic' text that rejects political action. Though it values both Hellenic spontaneity and free inquiry, and Hebraic conscience and rule-bound conduct, it maintains that Hellenism is more needed at present: 'Now, and for us, it is a time to Hellenise, and to praise knowing; for we have Hebraised too much, and have over-valued doing' (V: 255). The book also relegates politics more generally: for 'the believer in culture...public life and direct political action' are not '*much* permitted' (my emphasis: V: 226). Other similar statements encourage anti-political readings that see *Culture and Anarchy* as 'dissolving all social problems in a spiritual cloud'.[18] Where ideological readings that date from the 1970s maintain that its idea of 'the best self' disallows the class struggle of politics, more recent readings argue that it avoids the 'concrete bureaucracy' of the modern state, and that it values the free 'floating' of ideas at the expense of politics.[19] In opposition to such readings, it remains to indicate how Arnold attempts *indirect* political action through publicity. The political objectives of *Culture and Anarchy* are considered first here, before its own indirect political action.

Although this book upholds distance from political action in the interests of *more considered* action, it broadly promotes a more interventionist state that corresponds with 'the best self': 'what if we tried to rise above the idea of class to the idea of the whole community, *the State*, and to find our centre of light and authority there? Every one of us has the idea of the country, as a sentiment; hardly any one of us has the idea of *the State*, as a working power' (V: 134). Within *Culture and Anarchy*, the background of this passage lies in the Reform Act of 1867 which doubled the size of the electorate, and the riots in Hyde Park in London in the summer of 1866 that developed in a demonstration in support of reform. The iron railings of Hyde Park had then come down, and the call for the 'working power' of '*the State*' in the passage above seeks the maintenance of law and order.

The last chapter of *Culture and Anarchy*, 'Our Liberal Practitioners', presents a much less negative view of the state as it refutes criticisms that culture is committed merely to the free floating of ideas and, hence, that it is remote from politics. For this chapter seeks to show the process of 'Hellenizing' – 'the free spontaneous play of consciousness with which culture tries to float our stock habits of thinking and acting' (V: 220). This free play entails questioning the assumptions behind a series of proposed legislative measures, such as a change in inheritance law, and it results in specific political proposals – for instance, that the Irish Church should not be dis-established. Its specific political interests make this chapter at times seem addressed 'to our Liberal friends rejoicing in the possession of the talisman of free-trade' (V: 213). Individualistic, free-trade attitudes to social deprivation are here specifically rejected – the view of 'the *Times*, and our practical Liberal free-traders, and the British Philistines generally, that the increase of houses and manufactories, or the increase of population, are absolute goods in themselves' (V: 215). Though this chapter enjoins more collective responsibility for social well-being, and 'a frame of mind out of which the schemes of really fruitful reform may grow', its use of religious language (which permeates the whole of *Culture and Anarchy*) seems to have obscured its political import (V: 221). The evocation of a religious atmosphere was, however, common among politicians then. Moreover, since it appeals to high-mindedness, this religiosity may have some appeal to the Nonconformists whom Arnold otherwise undermines. 'Our Liberal Practitioners' first came out in two parts, in July and September, 1868, shortly before the dissolution of Parliament in November 1868. Overall, it supports a more national and egalitarian liberalism that is opposed to free trade, and, as the 1932 editor of *Culture and Anarchy* observed, it seems 'almost an electioneering pamphlet' (*C&A*, xxxi). The 'Preface' that Arnold wrote for the book after Gladstone's election and appointment as Prime Minister is a sustained attack on Gladstone's plans for the Irish Church. His integrative liberalism however accords with some of this government's many reform measures, that included increased state support of education.

Arnold's anti *laissez-faire* liberalism was reinforced by the indirect action of his writing. From the history of political thought, H.S. Jones points towards this indirect action. For besides acknowledging Arnold's broad support of reform measures and his '*liberal* critique of Victorian liberalism', Jones observes in passing that Arnold's liberal critique '*mobilised* a central notion in Victorian liberal thought, namely the primacy of the national as opposed to the merely sectional'[20] (my emphasis). Arnold's use of culture as a slogan, his personal attacks and his disinterested rhetoric contribute to this mobilizing effect, by undermining 'merely sectional' interests, including class interests. We have glimpsed the repetition of the term culture, through which it came to function as a counter to 'the talisman of free-trade' and 'philistine' narrowness – in other words, as a slogan for a broader liberalism that seeks a more integrated nation.

In its censorious name-calling, *Culture and Anarchy* further resembled contemporary politics, where publicity about individuals was used to mobilize political opinion. Most strikingly, *Culture and Anarchy* proposes that Lowe's notorious abuse of the working class as drunken and venal in his parliamentary speech against reform (in March 1866) arose 'in an agony of apprehension for his [Lowe's] Philistine or middle-class Parliament... now threatened with mixture and debasement' (V: 151). The reporting of Lowe's inflammatory speech in the press had been used to incite reform agitation nationally and he was widely identified as the chief Liberal opponent of democracy. In this public criticism of Lowe, Arnold sides with those who have suffered his attitudes. Through this ridicule, and the ridicule of other individuals – from a reader of the *British Banner* to particular Nonconformist ministers – he draws on the power of images and symbols to mobilize opinion. As much Liberal support nationally came from Nonconformity, his attempts to undermine Nonconformists – not only Nonconformist MP's such as Edward Miall – furthered his political aims.

This leads to Arnold's disinterested rhetoric, lastly. As a self-styled 'prophet of equality' in *Culture and Anarchy*, he criticizes individuals in all social classes. His even-handed demonstration of a 'best self' extends to his description of the strengths and weaknesses of each of the social classes, which are renamed as the barbarians (the aristocracy), the philistines (the middle class) and the populace (the working class). Not surprisingly, then, when readers today first encounter this criticism which comes from all sides, they tend to wonder what Arnold's own standpoint is. His levelling work seems contradicted in several displays of intense animosity – especially in a notorious passage in which the working-class 'rough' is seen as 'bawling as he likes, hustling as he likes' (V: 222). Such lines have been read as evidence of his own class anxiety as a middle-class critic. But his tactical, pragmatic approach to criticism, and his facility in imitation, make it equally seem that his expression of such sentiments indulges middle-class views in order to gain their support. The passage about the 'rough' 'bawling as he likes' significantly continues: 'Just as the rest of us, – as the country squires in the aristocratic class, as the political dissenters in the middle class, – he [the rough] has no idea of a *State'* (V: 222). To emphasize working-class unruliness is a pragmatic way of advancing the provision of education for the working class ('popular education') – by the modern state.

*Culture and Anarchy* thus abandons the distance that is kept from practice in political treatises. The usual, metaphysical topics of political discourse, such as the nature of political obligation, are absent in this book. In a political culture in which public image, attitudes and sensibility carry new weight, it uses manipulative publicity that depends on criticism of morals and manners. This writing in furtherance of a modern state hence comprises an irregular *Essay in Social and Political Criticism.* The challenge that *Culture and Anarchy* mounts lies not only in its explicit attack on materialism, narrow-mindedness and the 'practical operations' of free-trade Liberals, and its explicit support of a state that undermines the privileges of private property.

Arnold's mixing of different modes of publicity demonstrates some personal investment in the collapse of accepted hierarchies on his part, which at times aligns him with the new democracy. This investment appears fleetingly in a happy allusion to the present that recalls how the iron railings had come down in Hyde Park. Here, instead of being a source of alarm, 'the iron force of adhesion to the old routine – social, political, religious, – has wonderfully yielded; the iron force of exclusion of all which is new has wonderfully yielded' (V: 92). In such uneven publicity, Arnold's narrative persona appears alternately on the side of the 'rough' and opposed to him. His ambivalent position, which moves between old-world Enlightenment publicity and more disruptive forms, appears again in revealing lines at the end of his book. These grandiosely contemplate the 'real influence' that may accrue to a politician *or* a publicist, or someone who is both of these, on the new national stage:

> It may truly be averred . . . that at the present juncture the centre of movement is not in the House of Commons. It is in the fermenting mind of the nation; and his is for the next twenty years the real influence who can address himself to this. (V: 228)

# 4

## Postscript

> ...it is well for any great class and description of men in society to be able to say for itself what it wants, and not to have other classes, the so-called educated and intelligent classes, acting for it as its proctors, and supposed to understand what it wants and to provide for them. They really do not understand its wants, nor do they provide for them ('The Future of Liberalism', 1880, IX: 140).

Arnold's publicist activity did not end in 1869 although it became more straightforward as he took on the role of a modern critic of religion. This work got underway in his thinking about the Irish Church, where he newly addressed the restrictions that afflicted the Nonconformists. As his religious criticism went on to read the Bible as poetry, it elaborated his thinking about language and literature. The relativist understanding of language in this religious criticism conformed to his early claim, that 'everywhere there is connexion...no single event, no single literature, is adequately comprehended except in relation to other events, to other literatures' (I: 20–1).

The seriousness of his religious texts seems related to the deaths of two of Arnold's six children in 1868, and the chastening effects of criticisms of *Culture and Anarchy* that suggested that he had broken with good sense. When he returned to social and political criticism in the late 1870s he rarely used the term 'culture', which his writing had imbued with offensive, elitist associations. The elevation of his brother-in-law, W. E. Forster, to Minister of Education in1868 meant that he was unlikely to be promoted and it underscored his marginality.

Yet Arnold's books on *Saint Paul and Protestantism* (1870), *Literature and Dogma* (1873), *God and the Bible* (1875) and *Last*

*Essays on Church and Religion* (1877) brought him a new order of celebrity as readers reacted strongly to their insistence on Christianity's importance as a moral force despite the collapse of its religious truth. In 1877 he received invitations to stand for the Oxford Poetry Professorship again, and to become Rector of St. Andrews University, both of which he declined. He was, however, soon implicated in the spread of culture through the commodification of literature and new educational ventures. The demand for his criticism rested considerably on his reputation as a poet, and this was heightened by the publication of a selection of his poetry in 1878. As publishing houses became more implicated in commercial publicity, editors – some at his instigation – traded on his selections of writing from the eighteenth-century critic, Dr Johnson, and other English writers, including Wordsworth, Byron and Burke. Arnold's famous essay on 'The Study of Poetry' of 1880 was the introduction to T. H. Ward's *Lives of the English Poets*. As this essay begins with a long quotation from Arnold's contribution to a book in the year before, it underscores the repetition in his late criticism. His essays on particular writers broadly correspond with comments in his early poetry and private writing.

In his last decade he took on the role of a publicist on behalf of English literature. As the 'best ideas' and 'best knowledge' of Arnoldian culture now patently elided with investment in English literature where 'great' writers and 'great' men were in demand, his prose appeared in public-minded, nation-building undertakings. His concern with wide audiences and social integration can be glimpsed in his visit to the Ipswich Working Men's College in 1879. In the new publishing and educational contexts his criticism was typically occupied by ranking literary authors and texts, as a guide for uninitiated readers, much as newspaper books pages function today. More than many writers who are the subject of this 'Writers and their Work' series, he would have supported its ambition to make literature and criticism more accessible. By 1883, when he received a special state pension for his writing in poetry and literature, he had become a Victorian institution who was sought out for his name – most obviously, in the *Nineteenth Century* magazine.

From 1877 until his death in 1888 Arnold wrote nearly as much literary, political and social criticism as earlier in his career, over thirty essays, prefaces and addresses. Among his best known essays of this period, 'The Study of Poetry' reprises his earlier thinking on poetry though it is more insistent on poetry's future importance; 'Equality' develops his egalitarian views by opposing property inheritance; and 'Literature and Science' maintains the importance of literature and the humanities at a time when they seem threatened by science. Each of these essays speaks to issues that remain alive today. He also wrote on new literary subjects, such as the writer Ralph Waldo Emerson, for his two trips to America in the 1880s. On these trips he was regaled as a celebrity while he viewed democracy in practice and augmented his income through lecturing. At home in the 1880s, he spoke out more, and more directly, on party political matters – increasingly in opposition to Gladstone, often against Gladstone's use of the press.

The centrality of publicity to Arnold's political understanding is highlighted in one of his last essays, in 1887. Political life was then more dependent on journalism than in the 1860s, as Gladstone's career demonstrated. In reaction to the intense support for Gladstone in the *Pall Mall Gazette* at that time, Arnold refers to

> a new journalism which a clever and energetic man has lately invented. It has much to recommend it; it is full of ability, novelty, variety, sensation, sympathy, generous instincts . . . to get at the state of things as they truly are [it however] seems to feel no concern whatever (XI: 202).

As it upholds disinterested objectivity at the same time as it sensationally proposes that the *Pall Mall's* editor, W.T. Stead, has 'invented' 'a new journalism', this passage nicely illustrates Arnold's divided publicist identity.

---

This book has foregrounded the interrelationship of literature, education and politics in Arnold's path as a writer until 1869. A sense of language as a form of publicity is at the core of this account in which he moves from protest at the inadequacy of language to using publicity as a means of remaking society. Since he sought wholeness from the outset, there is some momentum in this movement, which was heightened by his work across the country and in Europe in the field of education.

Although Arnold has been at the centre of this discussion, his importance has rested on his openness to literature, ideas and Victorian institutions – Dr. Arnold, poetry, education, Oxford University, the civil service, journalism, politics and the public. His willingness to learn in a new culture of publicity is highlighted by the way that he arrived at the chapter headings of *Culture and Anarchy* from readers' use of his phrases from its first appearance as essays in journals. He came to write with a wide public and effectiveness in view, and publicity is fundamental to his liberalism.

The evolution of his ideas, and his concern with their realization, call for attention to the function of his writing at any one time. Rather than viewing him as a creative writer, or as a critic who is dedicated to social reform, this book has indicated how he combines these roles. These both appear in his use of his 'critical faculty' on the accountability that dominates modern politics. His resistance to the simple-minded imposition of 'payment by results' in the Revised Code illustrates the importance of the 'free spontaneous play of consciousness with which culture tries to float our stock habits of thinking and acting'. As importantly, his resistance suggests the value of criticism that is not merely academic, or merely literary, but which develops 'the art of the possible'.

# Notes

## INTRODUCTION

1. See, for example, Terry Eagleton's *Criticism and Ideology*, 104–10, and *The Function of Criticism*, 60–66; also Chris Baldick, *The Social Mission of English Criticism*, 18–60. Arnold appears as a rather less objectionable critic in criticism that focuses on the racial aspects of his thinking, following Robert Young, *Colonial Desire*.
2. For use of Arnoldian phrases, see eg. Francis Mulhern, *Culture/ Metaculture*, xvi, 28; on touchstones, Frank Kermode, *Pleasure and Change*, 39–42; on the obsolescence, Laurence Mazzeno, *Matthew Arnold*, 137.
3. Raymond Williams, *Culture and Society*, 136.
4. The most substantial, though controversial, account of the shift in publicity remains Jurgen Habermas, *The Structural Transformation of the Public Sphere*; for criticisms of Habermas, see Craig Calhoun, ed., *Habermas on the Public Sphere*.
5. Arnold's influence can be seen in the literary journalism of James Wood and AS Byatt, and in the fiction of Donna Tartt and Saul Bellow; the other Arnolds will appear in the course of this book.
6. Graham Holderness, 'Matthew Arnold: The Discourse of Criticism', 29.
7. Stephen Marcus, '*Culture and Anarchy* Today', 175.
8. Stefan Collini, ed., *Culture and Anarchy*, 'Introduction', especially xxvi;; also *Public Moralists*.

## CHAPTER 1. EARLY LIFE, POETRY AND PROSE, 1822–1853

1. K. & M. Allot, eds. *The Poems of Matthew Arnold*, 654: page references for the 'Preface' from this volume appear subsequently in the text.
2. Ian Hamilton's title, *A Gift Imprisoned*, suggests this shift from Romanticism; Park Honan, *Matthew Arnold*, proposes his turn from subjective feeling to banality and hard work in schools (247, 279).

My biography draws mainly on Hamilton, Honan, and Nicholas Murray, *A Life of Matthew Arnold*; also, Lionel Trilling, *Matthew Arnold*.

3. J. Hillis Miller, *The Disappearance of God*, 268, 265.

4. Quoted in David de Laura, *Hebrew and Hellene*, 15; for Newman's influence on Arnold, see 5–80.

5. See Franklin Court, *Institutionalising English Literature*, 106, and more generally, 85–118.

6. On the Arnold-Clough relationship see Bristow, ' "Love, let us be true to one another" '.

7. Hamilton, 105; see also Linda Ray Pratt, *Matthew Arnold Revisited*, 9.

8. Harold Bloom and Lionel Trilling, eds., *Victorian Prose and Poetry*, 580.

9. Thus Riede, 61, quotes U.C. Knoepflmacher.

10. Samuel Taylor Coleridge, quoted in Ben Knights, *The Idea of the Clerisy*, 52.

11. Aristotle, *Nicomachean Ethics*, 150.

12. Gage McWeeny, 'Crowd Management and the Science of Society' describes what is at issue as 'less a deep privacy than a collective communion', 105.

13. See D.J. Neff, '*The Times*, the Crimean War, and "Stanzas from the Grande Chartreuse" '.

14. Isobel Armstrong, *Victorian Scrutinies*, 34 , and more generally, 31–42.

15. On the context and reception of the 'Preface' see also Sydney Coulling, 23–50; on its democratic claims, see Mary Schneider, *Poetry for Democracy*, 51–5.

## CHAPTER 2. 'THE EMPIRE OF FACTS': INSPECTION, LECTURES AND CRITICISM UNTIL 1862

1. This chapter's historical account draws especially on J. W. Adamson, *English Education*; G. Kitson Clark, 'Statesman in Disguise'; Terry Eagleton, *The Function of Criticism*; Lauren M. E. Goodlad, *Victorian Literature and the Victorian State*; David Lloyd and Paul Thomas, *Culture and the State*; Jonathan Parry, *The Rise and Fall of Liberal Government*; Martin J. Wiener, *English Culture*. Also, R. H. Super's fine notes on Arnold's prose.

2. Raymond Williams' *Culture and Society* is discussed in Lloyd and Thomas, 14-19; also Collini, 'From Non-Fiction Prose to "Cultural Criticism" ', 14, 22–5.

3. Lloyd and Thomas, 117–118.

4. Quoted in Eagleton, 49–50.
5. Quoted in Adamson, 203.
6. See Schneider, 28–31, on Aristotelianism.
7. Aristotle, 150.
8. The Renaissance essayist, Michel de Montaigne, was himself steeped in classical sources.
9. Royle and Soper, 90.
10. Malcolm Woodfield, *A Victorian Spectator*, 157.
11. Quoted in Trilling, 223.
12. Woodfield, 11.
13. G. Saintsbury, *Matthew Arnold*, 71, 68.
14. Kermode, 86.
15. Michael Walzer, *Thick and Thin Moral Argument*, 6; see also H. S. Jones, *Victorian Political Thought*, 113, on the need for a return to ethical political thought.
16. See Marshall, *Contesting Cultural Rhetorics*, 69–71, 109–111.

## CHAPTER 3. 'THE THEATRE OF OPERATIONS': PUBLICITY, LITERATURE AND POLITICS, 1862–1869

1. T.S. Eliot, *The Sacred Wood*, 1.
2. Robert Young, *Colonial Desire*, 58; Mulhern, *Culture/Metaculture*, 174.
3. See Richard Salmon, 'A Simulacrum of Power'.
4. This account draws especially on Lucy Brown, *Victorian News and Newsapers*; Jurgen Habermas; Stephen Koss, *The Rise and Fall of the Political Press*, vol. one; Raymond Williams, *The Long Revolution*.
5. The sources of this political account include Catherine Hall, Keith McLelland and Jane Randall, *Defining the Victorian Nation*, 1–56 (especially on the period's historiography); John Thompson, *Political Scandal*; Eugenio Biagini, *Gladstone*; Patrick Joyce, *Democratic Subjects*; Stephen Koss; Jonathan Parry, *The Rise and Fall of Liberal Government* (especially 178–194).
6. See Pierre Bourdieu, 'The Field of Cultural Production', 53.
7. Patrick Joyce, *Democratic Subjects*, 4–5; 136–7.
8. On Arnold's ambitions and frustration, see Patrick Jackson, *Education Act Forster*, 46–48.
9. Quoted in Adamson, 230.
10. On 'liberal heroics', see David Wayne Thomas, *Cultivating Victorians*, 7, 9–14.
11. Quoted in Coulling, 119.
12. See Amanda Anderson, 'Disinterestedness as a Vocation', on which the following account draws.

13. Mark Hampton, *Visions of the Press*, 106–108.
14. See Susan Walsh, 'That Arnoldian Wragg'.
15. Bourdieu, *Distinction*, 444.
16. On these issues see, for instance, Ryle and Soper, *To Relish the Sublime?*
17. Morris Dickstein, *Double Agent*, 9.
18. Baldick, 36.
19. Terry Eagleton's *Criticism and Ideology* set in train the ideological readings, for instance by Baldick. See more recently, Goodlad, 156, on Arnold and the state; and Thomas, 37, on the free-floating ideas: these and other recent American critics approach the idea of 'the best self' less dismissively, in relation to the ethical significance of disinterestedness.
20. See Jones, *Victorian Political Thought*, 65.

# Select Bibliography

## WRITING BY MATTHEW ARNOLD

*Complete Prose Works* of Matthew Arnold, ed. R. H. Super, Vols. I-XI (Ann Arbor: University of Michigan Press, 1960–1977).

*Culture and Anarchy: An Essay in Social and Political Criticism* by Matthew Arnold, ed. John Dover Wilson (Cambridge: Cambridge University Press, 1988 [1932]).

*The Letters of Matthew Arnold*, ed. Cecil Lang, Vols. 1–6 (Charlottesville, Va.: University Press of Virginia, 1996–2001).

*The Letters of Matthew Arnold to Arthur Hugh Clough*, ed. H.F. Lowry (Oxford: Clarendon Press, 1932).

*The Notebooks of Matthew Arnold*, eds. Karl Young and Hilary Waldo Dunn, (London and New York: Oxford University Press, 1952).

*Parliamentary Papers: Reports of HM Inspectors of Schools*. 1852: LXXX.

*Passages from the Prose Writings of Matthew Arnold* (London: Smith Elder, 1880).

*The Poems of Matthew Arnold*, eds. Kenneth Allott and Miriam Allott (London and New York: Longman, 1979, [1965]).

*Reports on Elementary Schools*, ed. F. Sandford (London: Macmillan, 1889).

*The Yale Manuscript*, ed. S.O.A. Ullmann (Ann Arbor: University Press of Michigan, 1989).

## BIBLIOGRAPHIES

See also internet sources, especially MLA; also *Victorian Poetry* for annual updates.

Machon, Clinton, *The Essential Matthew Arnold: An Annotated Bibliography of Modern Studies* (New York: G.K. Hall, 1993).

———, 'Matthew Arnold: The Year's Work', *Victorian Poetry* 43, 3 (Fall 2005).

Mazzeno, Laurence W., *Matthew Arnold: The Critical Legacy* (New York,

Rochester and Woodbridge: Camden House, 1999). A useful, broad update, whose chronological structure foregrounds Arnold's role as a touchstone for shifting critical currents.

## BIOGRAPHIES AND BIOGRAPHICAL-CRITICAL STUDIES OF ARNOLD

Collini, Stefan, *Matthew Arnold: A Critical Portrait* (Oxford: Oxford University Press, 1994 [1988]). Elucidation of Arnold's different types of criticism in a sympathetic study that foregrounds 'the Arnoldian voice' and temper.

Hamilton, Ian, *A Gift Imprisoned* (London: Bloomsbury Publishing, 1998). Lively biography devoted to the years of Arnold's best poetry and the issue of its decline.

Honan, Park, *Matthew Arnold* (London: Weidenfeld & Nicholson, 1981). Although weighted towards the poetry, this perceptive account remains the best all-round biography, and a valuable account of the intellectual and literary influences on its subject.

Lowry, Howard Forster, ed., Introduction, *The Letters of Matthew Arnold to Arthur Hugh Clough* (Oxford: Clarendon Press, 1932). Worth reading still, especially for its awareness of Arnold's political interests.

Machin, Clifford, *Matthew Arnold: A Literary Life* (Basingstoke: Macmillan, 1998). This moves away from customary attention to the intellectual and literary influences on Arnold's development to its social and professional contexts, though it neglects Arnold's educational work.

Murray, Nicholas, *A Life of Matthew Arnold* (London: Hodder & Stoughton, 1996). A supplement to Honan's study, with a stronger sense of Arnold's worldliness.

Pratt, Linda Ray, *Matthew Arnold Revisited* (New York: Twayne Publishers, 2000). Revision of Arnold's development as a writer in the light of post-structuralist linguistic emphasis, with useful chapter on his religious criticism; predominantly occupied with the poetry.

Trilling, Lionel, *Matthew Arnold* (London: George Allen & Unwin, 1955 [1939]). A suggestive and influential study that contextualizes the development of a liberal mind with notable reference to contemporary politics as well as ideas.

## CONTEMPORARY CRITICISM OF ARNOLD AND OTHER PRIMARY SOURCES

Aristotle, *The Nicomachean Ethics*, translated by J.A.K. Thomson, revised by Hugh Tredennick (London: Penguin Books, 2004 [1955]).

Arnold, Thomas, 'The Oxford Malignants and Dr. Hampden', *The Edinburgh Review*, Vol. 63, (April 1836), 225–239.

Armstrong, Isobel, *Victorian Scrutinies: Reviews of Poetry 1830–1870* (London: Athlone Press, 1972). Extracts from criticism on key debates.

Dawson, Carl, ed., *Matthew Arnold: the Poetry*. The Critical Heritage (London: Routledge & Kegan Paul, 1973).

Dawson, Carl, and Pfordresher, eds., *Matthew Arnold: Prose Writings. The Critical Heritage* (London: Routledge, 1995).

Saintsbury, George, *Matthew Arnold* (London: William Blackwood, 1899). A sympathetic fin-de-siècle study that stresses Arnold's skills as a writer and his influence.

Stanley, A.P., *Life of Thomas Arnold, D.D.* (London: Ward, Lock & Co., 1910 [1844]).

Woodfield, Malcolm, *A Victorian Spectator: Uncollected Writings of R.H. Hutton* (Bristol: Bristol Press, 1989).

## CRITICAL AND CONTEXTUAL STUDIES WITH REFERENCE TO ARNOLD

### Books and Discussion within Books

Adamson, John William, *English Education: 1789–1902* (Cambridge: Cambridge University Press, 1930). Invaluable background to the introduction of the Revised Code, with some slight mention of Arnold.

Anderson, Amanda, *The Powers of Distance: Cosmopolitanism and the Cultivation of Detachment* (Princeton, NJ., and Oxford: Princeton University Press, 2001). Significant reassessment of status of Arnoldian disinterestedness, in the context of current re-evaluation of liberalism.

Armstrong, Isobel, *Victorian Scrutinies: Reviews of Poetry 1830-1870* (London: Athlone Press, 1972). Lucid contextual exposition and analysis accompanies extracts of contemporary poetic thinking.

——, *Victorian Poetry: Poetry, Poetics and Politics* (London: Routledge, 1993). Includes fine, contextualized exploration of Arnold in crisis at mid-century.

Arac, Jonathan, *Critical Genealogies: Historical Situations for Postmodern Literary Studies* (Guildford and New York: Columbia University Press, 1987). Helpful discussion of Arnold's appropriation within American English Studies, with a post-structuralist reading of the sources of his power and his 'empty' language.

Baldick, Chris, *The Social Mission of English Criticism 1848–1932* (New York and Oxford: Clarendon Press, 1987 [1983]). Influential study of Arnold's ideological importance in the institutionalization of English teaching in England.

Bell, Bill, 'From Parnassus to Grub Street', in Elizabeth James, ed., *Macmillan: A Publishing Tradition* (Basingstoke: Palgrave, 2002), 52–69. Timely examination of Arnold's relations with his publishers and his attitude towards the marketplace.

Bristow, Joseph, ed., *The Cambridge Companion to Victorian Poetry* (Cambridge: Cambridge University Press, 2000). Some perceptive discussion of Arnold and useful contextualization.

Brown, E.K., *Matthew Arnold: A Study in Conflict* (Hamden, Conn.: Archon Books, 1966 [1948]). An important, acute account that turns on Arnold's allegiances to both disinterestedness and practicality.

Collini, Stefan, *Public Moralists: Political Thought and Intellectual Life in Britain 1850-1930* (Oxford and New York: Oxford University Press, 1993 [1991]). Judicious, influential exploration of the moral basis of Victorian thought.

——, ed., *Arnold: Culture and Anarchy and Other Writings*, by Matthew Arnold (Cambridge and New York: Cambridge University Press, 2004 [1993]). A useful collection of Arnold's writing on political topics whose Introduction foregrounds his methods and their subsequent currency.

——, 'From 'Non-Fiction Prose' to 'Cultural Criticism', in Juliet John and Alice Jenkins, eds., *Rethinking Victorian Culture* (Basingstoke: Macmillan, 2000; New York: St. Martin's Press, 2000), 13–28. A helpful account of the fortunes of 'non-fiction prose' which bear on Arnold's academic presence.

Connell, W.F., *The Educational Thought of Matthew Arnold* (London: Routledge, 1998 [1950]). Detailed factual information that accords with later accounts.

Coulling, Sydney, *Matthew Arnold and his Critics: A Study of Arnold's Controversies* (Athens: Ohio University Press, 1974). A useful study that demonstrates Arnold's responsiveness and flexibility.

Corbett, Mary Jean, *Allegorising Union in Irish and English Writing 1790-1870: Politics, History and the Family from Edgeworth to Arnold* (Cambridge: Cambridge University Press, 2000). A timely section on Arnold argues that he reconstituted dissatisfaction with the Anglo-Irish Union in terms of England's problematic 'character';

108

and that he tried to defuse anti-Irish feeling (151–70).

Court, Franklin, *Institutionalising English Literature: The Culture and Politics of Literary Study 1750-1900* (Stanford, California: Stanford University Press, 1994). Arnold's connections with faculty at London University are foregrounded in this account that maintains his own relative unimportance for nineteenth-century University English.

Culler, A. Dwight, *Imaginative Reason: the Poetry of Matthew Arnold* (New Haven and London: Yale University Press, 1996). A close study that foregrounds the intertextual and elegaic quality of Arnold's poetry.

De Laura, David J., *Hebrew and Hellene in Victorian England: Newman, Arnold and Pater* (Austin and London: University of Texas Press, 1969). An important, substantial study of Newman's intellectual influence on Arnold.

——, ed., *Matthew Arnold: a Collection of Critical Essays* (Englewood Cliffs, N. J.: Prentice-Hall, 1973). An introduction to Arnold's poetry and the issues it raises, which includes T.S. Eliot's essay on Arnold and Walter Pater.

Dickstein, Morris, *Double Agent: the Critic and Society*, (New York and Oxford: Oxford University Press, 1992). Arnold's allegiance to knowing *and* doing, art *and* society, timelessness *and* timeliness, receive rare consideration in a wide-ranging text that maintains the importance of general criticism.

Douglas-Fairhurst, Robert, *Victorian Afterlives: The Shaping of Influence in Nineteenth-Century Literature* (Oxford and New York: Oxford University Press, 2004 [2002]). Slight yet deft attention to Arnold's thinking about influence.

Eagleton, Terry, *Criticism and Ideology: A Study in Marxist Literary Theory* (London and New York: Verso, 1992 [1975]). This book's account of the attempt to co-opt the working-classes politically in Arnold's 'Democracy', within a European-wide discussion, initiated further ideological readings of his work.

——, *The Function of Criticism: From 'The Spectator' to Post-structuralism* (London: Verso, 1996 [1984]). In the wake of Habermas, a study of English criticism and the public sphere that aligns Arnold with the academic sphere.

Eliot, T.S., *The Sacred Wood: Essays on Poetry and Criticism* (London: Methuen, 1972 [1920]). An influential collection in which Arnold is a significant presence although there is little sustained attention to him.

Goodlad, Lauren M.E., *Victorian Literature and the Victorian State* (Baltimore: Johns Hopkins University Press, 2003). The registration of Arnold's 'dematerialised idea' of the state in this study suffers from neglect of his civil service employment and Liberal political life.

Hall, Catherine, Keith McLelland and Jane Rendall, *Defining the Victorian Nation: Class, Race, Gender and the Reform Act of 1867* (Cambridge and New York: Cambridge University Press, 2000). A good introduction to the period's historiography; following Young, discussion of Arnold here centres on his belief in racial regeneration more than his attitudes to class.

Hardman, Graham, *Six Victorian Thinkers* (Manchester: Manchester University Press, 1991). Deft attention to the reticence of Arnold's poetry in a chapter that nonetheless registers its Keatsian aspects.

Holderness, Graham, 'Matthew Arnold: The Discourse of Criticism', in Gary Day, ed., *The British Critical Tradition: a re-evaluation*, (Basingstoke: Macmillan, 1993), 29–37. Some recognition of Arnold as a publicist and strategist in a chapter that considers his importance for English criticism.

Houghton, Walter, 'Periodical Literature and the Articulate Classes', in Joanne Shattock and Michael Woolf, eds., *The Victorian Periodical Press: Samplings and Soundings*, (Leicester: Leicester University Press, 1982), 3–27. Assessment of the importance of the 1860s periodical press in the light of Arnold's attack on its sectarianism.

Hunter, Ian, *Culture and Government: The Emergence of Literary Education* (Basingstoke: Macmillan, 1988). This bureaucratic and technological reading of the 'emergence' of literary teaching disputes Arnold's central role in accounts of 'the rise of English' by Baldick and others.

Jackson, Patrick, *Education Act Forster: A Political Biography of W.E. Forster, 1818–1886* (Madison, New Jersey: Fairleigh Dickinson University; London: Associated University Presses, 1997). Some useful attention to the relationship between Forster and Arnold.

Jacoby, Russell, *The End of Utopia: Politics and Culture in an Age of Apathy* (New York: Basic Books, 1999). In this book that deplores a current lack of utopian spirit Arnold appears as an exemplary critical democrat.

Jones, H.S., *Victorian Political Thought* (Basingstoke: Macmillan Press, 2000). Timely advance of Arnold's claims as a political thinker, a liberal critic of Victorian liberalism.

Kermode, Frank, with Geoffrey Hartman, John Guillory and Carey Perloff, ed. Robert Alter, *Pleasure and Change: The Aesthetics of Canon* (Oxford and New York: Oxford University Press, 2004). There is frequent return to Arnold's 'touchstones' in this discussion of the canon in terms of pleasure and change.

Knights, Ben, *The Idea of the Clerisy* (Cambridge: Cambridge University Press, 1978). Useful Coleridgean grounding of Arnold's thinking, even though this appears unduly inflexible in this study.

Lane, Christopher, 'The Arnoldian Ideal, or Cultural Studies and the Problem of Nothingness', 283–311, in Amanda Anderson and Joseph Valente, eds., *Disciplinarity at the Fin de Siècle* (Princeton, N.J.: Princeton UP, 2002). Thoughtful discussion of the sense of nothingness in Arnold's writing.

Lipman, Samuel, ed., *Culture and Anarchy* (New Haven and London: Yale University Press, 1994). This includes essays on this text's late twentieth-century importance by Lipman, Maurice Cowling, Gerald Graff and Stephen Marcus.

Lloyd, David, and Thomas, Paul, *Culture and the State* (London and New York: Routledge, 1998). A substantial revision of oppositional approaches to 'culture and society' that delineates the complicity of culture and the state for Arnold.

Malachuk, Daniel S., *Perfection, the State, and Victorian Liberalism* (Basingstoke and New York: Palgrave Macmillan, 2005). Another text that turns to Arnold and also to John Stuart Mill, as a Victorian liberal writer who has continuing relevance – here in terms of a perfectionism and statism that resist scepticism.

Marcus, Steven, 'Culture and Anarchy Today', in Samuel Lipman, ed., *Culture and Anarchy*, 165–85. An essay that ably points up the difficulties and continuing value of *Culture and Anarchy* in modern multicultural societies.

Marshall, Margaret, *Contesting Cultural Rhetorics: Public Discourse and Education*, (Ann Arbor: University of Michigan Press, 1995). A long critical section discusses Arnold's attempts to persuade his readers in 'Democracy', a text that became central to American educational debates in the 1890s.

Meisel, Perry, *The Myth of the Modern: A Study in British Literature and Criticism After 1850* (New Haven and London: Yale University Press, 1987). This includes perceptive discussion of Arnold's movement from a literal-minded poetry to criticism that is extraordinarily literary.

Miller, J. Hillis, *The Disappearance of God: Five Nineteenth-Century Writers* (Cambridge, Mass.: Harvard University Press, 1963; London: Oxford University Press, 1963). This book on Victorian religious experience includes one of the most influential accounts of Arnold, in which spiritual loss is the defining experience of his writing.

——, *The Linguistic Moment: From Wordsworth to Stevens* (Princeton, N.J.: Princeton University Press, 1985). A deconstructive reading of Arnold's use of language that maintains its lack of fixed reference.

Mulhern, Francis, *Culture/Metaculture* (London and New York: Routledge, 2000). The fleeting references to Arnold in this book that traces thinking about culture are symptomatic of continuing impatience with Arnold among English cultural critics.

Riede, David, *Matthew Arnold and the Betrayal of Language* (Charlottes-ville, Va.; Virginia University Press, 1988). An important decon-structive account, that reads Arnold's earlier poetry in terms of the clear distinction between poetic and scientific language in his religious criticism of the 1870s.

Rothblatt, Sheldon, *Tradition and Change in English Liberal Education: an Essay in History and Culture* (London: Faber & Faber, 1976). An able broad account, that freshly contextualized Arnold in higher education.

Royle, Chris, and Kate Soper, *To Relish the Sublime? Culture and Self-Realisation in Postmodern Times* (London and New York: Verso, 2002). Arnold's association of culture as universal self-realization has a central place in this sympathetic interdisciplinary study of the history of this ideal.

Schneider, Mary, *Poetry in the Age of Democracy: The Literary Criticism of Matthew Arnold* (Lawrence, Kansas: University of Kansas Press, 1989). This book, which considers particular influences on Arnold, including Aristotle, argues that his literary criticism is directed to a democratic society.

Stone, Donald, *Communications with the Future: Matthew Arnold in Dialogue* (Ann Arbor: University of Michigan Press, 1997). An off-putting approach to Arnold through many subsequent thinkers – yet the chapter on 'Arnold and the Pragmatists' (139–74) im-portantly broaches Arnold's belief in action and democracy.

Thomas, David Wayne, *Cultivating Victorians: Liberal Culture and the Aesthetic* (Philadelphia, Pennsylvania; University of Pennsylvania Press, 2004). This book illustrates the current interest in liberalism, especially in liberal disinterestedness, and hence in Arnold – in whom, for Thomas, disinterestedness takes the form of an apolitical 'many sidedness'.

Trilling, Lionel, and Bloom, Harold, eds., *Victorian Prose and Poetry* (Oxford: Oxford University Press, 1973). Worth attention for assessments of Arnold's prose and poetry that were broadly representative of literary judgements at the time.

Turner, Frank W., *Contesting Cultural Authority: Essays in Victorian Intellectual Life* (Cambridge: Cambridge University Press, 1993). Some useful attention to Arnold's Hellenism, in relation to Victorian idealism; also to the differences in twentieth-century approaches to Victorian literature across the Atlantic.

Venuti, Lawrence, *The Translator's Invisibility: A History of Translation* (London and New York: Routledge, 1995). An influential study that argues Arnold's repression of cultural differences in his work on Homer, in contrast to the popular freight of Francis Newman's 'foreignising translation' (129–146).

Williams, Raymond, *Culture and Society* (Harmondsworth and New York: Penguin, 1985 [1958]). Nuanced reading of Arnold that acknowledges his practical bearings, in an influential oppositional account of culture and society.

Young, Robert J.C., *Colonial Desire: Hybridity in Theory, Culture and Race* (London and New York: Routledge, 1996). Important re-examination of Arnold's racial thinking.

## Articles

A very select list. *Victorian Poetry* is worth special mention as it regularly features articles on Arnold's poetry; and again, see the MLA on the internet.

Bristow, Joseph, '"Love, Let us Be True to One Another": Matthew Arnold, Arthur Hugh Clough, and "Our Aqueous Ages"', *Literature and History* 4, no.1 (1995 Spring), 27–49.

Hawkes, Terence, 'The Heimlich Manoevre', *Textual Practice* 8, no. 2 (1994 Summer), 302–16.

McWeeny, Gage, 'Crowd Management and the Science of Society', *Victorian Poetry*, 41, 1 (Spring 2003), 93–111.

Neff, D.J., '*The Times*, the Crimean War, and "Stanzas from the Grande Chartreuse"', *Journal for Scholars and Critics of Language and Literature* 33, no. 2 (Spring 1997), 169–81.

Pinkney, Tony, 'Matthew Arnold and the Subject of Modernity', *Critical Survey* No. 3 (1992), 226–32.

Walsh, Susan, 'That Arnoldian Wragg: Anarchy as Menstrosity in Victorian Social Criticism', *Victorian Literature and Culture* 20 (1992), 217-41.

## FURTHER HISTORICAL AND THEORETICAL STUDIES

Altick, R.D., *The English Common Reader: a Social History of the Mass Reading Public, 1800–1900* (Chicago, Ill.: University of Chicago Press, 1998 [1957]).

Biagini, Eugenio, *Gladstone* (Basingstoke: Macmillan, 2000; New York: St. Martin's Press, 2000).

Bourdieu, Pierre, *Distinction: A Social Critique of the Judgement of Taste*, tr. Richard Nice (London and New York: Routledge, 1989 [c1984]).

——, The Field of Cultural Production: Essays on Art and Literature ed. Randal Johnson (Cambridge: Polity, 1993).

Brown, Lucy, *Victorian News and Newspapers* (Oxford: Clarendon, 1985).

Brake, Laurel, ed., *Subjugated Knowledges: Journalism, Gender and Literature in The Nineteenth Century* (Basingstoke: Macmillan, 1994).

Calhoun, Craig, ed., *Habermas on the Public Sphere* (Cambridge, Mass. and London: MIT Press, 1992).

Clark, G. Kitson, 'Statesmen in Disguise: Reflections on the History and Neutrality of the Civil Service', *Historical Journal*, II, I, 1959: 19–40.

Crowley, Tony, *The Politics of Discourse: The Standard Language Question in British Cultural Debates* (Basingstoke: Macmillan Education, 1989).

Habermas, Jurgen, *The Structural Transformation of the Public Sphere*, tr. Thomas Burger, asstd. Frederick Lawrence (Cambridge: Polity, 1992 [1962]).

Hampton, Mark, *Visions of the Press in Britain, 1850–1950* (Urbana, Illinois: University of Illinois Press, 2004).

Haskell, Thomas L., ed., *The Authority of Experts: Studies in History and Theory* (Bloomington: Indiana University Press, 1984).

Joyce, Patrick, *Democratic Subjects: The Self and the Social in Nineteenth-Century England* (Cambridge: Cambridge University Press, 1994).

Koss, Stephen, *The Rise and Fall of the Political Press in Britain* (London: Hamish Hamilton, 1981), vol. 1.

Lee, A.J., *The Origins of the Popular Press in England, 1855–1914* (London: Croom Helm, 1976).

Parry, Jonathan *The Rise and Fall of Liberal Government in Victorian Britain* (New Haven and London: Princeton UP, 1993).

Perkin, Harold, *Rise of Professional Society: England since 1880* (London: Routledge, 1989).

Richards, T., *The Commodity Culture of Victorian England: Advertising and Spectacle, 1851–1914* (London and New York: Verso, 1991 [1990]).

Salmon, Richard, 'A Simulacrum of Power: Intimacy and Abstraction in the Rhetoric of the New Journalism', in Laurel Brake, Bill Bell and David Finkelstein, eds., *Nineteenth-Century Media and the Construction of Identities* (Basingstoke and New York: Palgrave, 2000), 27–39.

Thompson, John, *Political Scandal: Power and Visibility in the Media Age* (Cambridge and Malden, Mass.: Polity, 2000).

Thompson, F.M.L., *The Rise of Respectable Society: A Social History of Victorian Britain, 1830–1900* (London: Fontana, 1988).

Walzer, Michael, *Thick and Thin: Moral Argument at Home and Abroad* (Notre Dame and London: Notre Dame University Press, 1994).

Wiener, Martin J., *English Culture and the Decline of the Industrial Spirit: 1850–1980* (Harmondsworth: Penguin, 1985 [1981]).

Williams, Raymond, *The Long Revolution* (Harmondsworth: Pelican, 1984 [1961]).

# Index

115

www.ingramcontent.com/pod-product-compliance
Lightning Source LLC
Chambersburg PA
CBHW020702030726
47498CB00002B/602